TEACHING ENGLISH IN THE NA

LANGUAGE, LITERACY AND GENDER

Hilary Minns

Series Editor: Patrick Scott

Hodder & Stoughton

LONDON SYDNEY AUCKLAND TORONTO

ACKNOWLEDGMENTS

I would like to thank the following people for their help in sharing ideas and experiences with me: Michelle Bayliss, Beryl Glasscoe, Gill Kirkham, Val Millman, Carole Sellors, Graham Sellors, Barbara Slater, Stewart Scott, Carolyn Steedman.

I would also like to thank Jo Finigan and Win Kelly, of Hearsall Community Primary School, Coventry, for talking to me about the work staff and parents undertook in classifying books, and for allowing me to use this work as an example of good practice.

I am particularly grateful to Saras Fry, Brian Morley, Barbara Thomas and Sandra Shipton of Edgewick Community Primary School, Coventry, for talking to me about their equal opportunities policy, letting me observe an early-years class in their 'railway station', and for allowing me to describe their gender-based work which appears in *Gender Equality: Five Schools' Experience of Change*.

Finally, of course, I need to thank the children whose work appears here and who have shown how energetically and enthusiastically they can take on gender issues for themselves.

I am grateful to Coventry Local Education Authority for permission to quote from their excellent booklet *Gender Equality: Five Schools' Experience of Change*.

The Publishers would like to thank the following for permission to reproduce material in this volume:
Paul Buttle, for his letter from The Sun to Zoe; The Press Council (now the Press Complaints Commission) for the letter to Zoe and Sharron.

British Library Cataloguing in Publication Data
Minns, Hilary
   Language, literacy and gender: equal opportunities
in primary English. – (TEINC)
I. Title   II. Series
372.6

   ISBN 0–340–54843–6

First published 1991

Produced by Serif Tree, Kidlington, Oxon
Printed in Great Britain for the educational publishing division of Hodder & Stoughton Ltd, Mill Road, Dunton Green, Sevenoaks, Kent by St Edmundsbury Press, Bury St Edmunds, Suffolk.

TEACHING EN

LANGI

Please renew/return this item by the last date shown.

So that your telephone call is charged at local rate,
please call the numbers as set out below: 2

	From Area codes 01923 or 0208:	From the rest of Herts:
Renewals:	01923 471373	01438 737373
Enquiries:	01923 471333	01438 737333
Minicom:	01923 471599	01438 737599

L32b

CONTENTS

Introduction

Every teacher who recognises the need for equal opportunities and who tries to bring about change in the classroom becomes part of the movement towards equality and self-fulfilment not only in schools but within society too. My own history of concern and action for equal opportunities is embedded within the primary schools that were part of my teaching life in the 1970s and 1980s. It was clear that some of the staff shared a desire to bring about change, both for ourselves and for the children we taught; we joined groups, read books and went to conferences. We made changes in our classrooms, we talked to parents and colleagues, and above all we talked to each other and supported each other.

Schools and their Governing Bodies now have a legal obligation to reduce sex-differentiation in their schools, and though there are many influences beyond the school gates – class, race, culture, the media – these do not need to hinder schools in setting their own agenda for equality and providing opportunities for girls and boys to experience the freedom to learn about themselves and their place within society.

The National Curriculum recognises that each pupil is entitled to a broad curriculum regardless of race, gender, disability or geographical location[1]. Indeed, the Secretary of State's original proposals carried a clear directive about the importance of equal opportunities, something that might seem surprising in a subject-centred curriculum which is not specifically geared to the learning needs of individual students:

> Issues of equal opportunity may arise in a number of contexts, for example, those of gender, race, disability and religion. Such issues must be a concern of those devising the National Curriculum because the attainment targets and programmes of study must not be biased, deliberately or unwittingly, towards or against any such group[2].

Statements like this underlie National Curriculum policy and give us good reason to re-examine our classroom practice, particularly in areas like English teaching, where discrimination can be powerfully felt.

This book is written for primary school teachers and teachers-in-training who are interested in devising and implementing schemes of work in English which take account of gender-based equal opportunities, and at the same time meet the requirements of the National Curriculum. It uses examples of good practice to show how the Programmes of Study for Key Stages 1 and 2 can be used creatively to underpin successful teaching in English and suggests ways of formulating whole-school policies in order to promote equality and reduce gender-related underachievement.

CHAPTER 1

The Historical Perspective

Let's begin by considering Sophy. Sophy, you may recall, is the girl Rousseau creates in *Emile* to be Emile's helpmate throughout life[3]. She is by nature frivolous, simpering and silly, as all girls are, and is therefore subordinate to Emile in every way, but she is also of considerable importance to him because her function is to entertain, serve and please him. She is of course not to receive the same kind of education Rousseau proposes for Emile; indeed, she is not to receive any education for, as a girl, she is impossible to educate.

Two hundred years ago Mary Wollstonecraft was by no means alone in reacting angrily to Rousseau's dismissal of female intelligence and education and, in her seminal *A Vindication of the Rights of Woman*, she pointed an accusing finger at damaging child-rearing practices which condemned a girl 'to sit for hours together listening to the idle chat of weak nurses, or to attend at her mother's toilet'. Little wonder, she argued, 'that she will imitate her mother or aunts, and amuse herself by adorning her lifeless doll, as they do in dressing her.' Girls, she says, have learnt to behave this way since they are allowed no other outlet for their energy or imagination. But, she contends:

> a girl, whose spirits have not been damped by inactivity, or innocence tainted by false shame, will always be a romp, and the doll will never excite attention unless confinement allows her no alternative.[4]

As the eldest sister in a family of three girls, a former governess and headmistress in a girls' school, Wollstonecraft's ideas on the education of girls and boys were rooted in practical wisdom. 'In an elementary day-school,' she advised, 'boys and girls, the rich and poor, should meet together.' What we now understand as equality of opportunity within a broad and balanced curriculum, and teaching methods which promote active learning in a healthy environment, she describes in 1792 like this:

> to prevent any of the distinctions of vanity, [boys and girls] should be dressed alike, and all obliged to submit to the same discipline, or leave the school. The school-room ought to be surrounded by a large piece of ground, in which the children might be usefully exercised, for at this age they should not be confined to any

sedentary employment for more than an hour at a time. But these relaxations might all be rendered a part of elementary education, for many things improve and amuse the senses, when introduced as a kind of show, to the principles of which, dryly laid down, children would turn a deaf ear. For instance, botany, mechanics, and astronomy. Reading, writing, arithmetic, natural history, and some simple experiments in natural philosophy, might fill up the day; but these pursuits should never encroach on gymnastic plays in the open air. The elements of religion, history, the history of man, and politics, might also be taught by conversations, in the socratic form.[5]

And it was in 1825, thirty-three years after the publication of Wollstonecraft's book, that William Thompson published his *Appeal of One Half of the Human Race, Women, Against the Pretensions of the Other Half, Men, To Retain Them in Political, and Thence In Civil and Domestic Slavery*[6] in which he stated:

> You look forward to a better aspect of society, where restless and anxious individual competition shall give place to mutual co-operation and joint possession; where individuals in large numbers, male and female, forming voluntary associations, shall become a mutual guarantee to each other for the supply of all equal wants.

It should be becoming clear now that the debate about sexual equality is not new; but visionary ideals like Wollstonecraft's and Thompson's have a habit of getting lost, distorted or repressed across generations, only to resurface at moments of significant change – in times of war, perhaps, or of economic and social upheaval. And what one generation takes for granted is easily lost and has to be rediscovered and relearnt by future generations.

Such a time of loss was felt by the middle of the nineteenth century, when many women and their daughters became constrained by a life of domesticity; the model of the perfect woman as homemaker, wife and mother was eulogised in Coventry Patmore's 'The Angel in the House':

> Her sons pursue the butterflies,
> Her baby daughter mocks the doves
> With throbbing coo; in his fond eyes
> She's Venus with her little Loves.

Little girls who spent their days gently mocking doves found the stories of their lives already mapped out for them in literature like this and in the fairy tales they were given to read. The late eighteenth century and early nineteenth century was a period when the male collectors of folk and fairy tales, followers of the Grimm brothers and Perrault, made their collections of stories; what eventually came to be written down by them and handed on to little Victorian girls in published form, were the tales of passive, beautiful heroines, waiting to be rescued, to be approved. In her introduction to *Clever Gretchen and Other Forgotten Folktales*[8] Alison Lurie reminds us:

> There are thousands of folktales in the world that are not at all like this. They have heroines who can fight and hunt as well as any man, heroines who defeat giants, answer riddles, outwit the Devil, and rescue their friends and relatives from all sorts of dangers and evil spells.
>
> Why don't we know these stories as well as the others? It is because the first collections of fairy tales for children were put together over a hundred years ago, when women and girls were supposed to be weak and helpless; and the editors who picked the stories out of the many that were available chose ones like 'Snow White', 'Cinderella', 'Sleeping Beauty', and 'Little Red Riding Hood'. These tales were printed over and over again, while the rest were almost forgotten.

Alison Lurie has collected and retold some of these forgotten tales in her book and shows how Clever Gretchen, Kate Crackernuts, Maid Maleen and the other heroines of the stories, use their courage and resourcefulness to turn despair and ill-fortune into hope and promise for the future.

But let us now take the story forward a hundred years, as they do in the old tales, and see what is happening in the middle of our own century. The Second World War brought with it changes in the lives of millions of people. Female employment in factories helped women towards a new identity, towards feelings of self-worth. A former welder in the film *Rosie the Riveter* looks back to those times when a new kind of heroine was created:

> We believed we were 'the New Woman'. We were a really smart-looking group of ladies . . . and we all loved one another. Men had been telling us all along the line, oh it takes fifty years to become a welder, but it wasn't true at all. I liked the welding because it was a special thing and at the end of the day I always felt I'd accomplished something. There was a product, there was something to be seen.

When the war was over, women across Europe and the States were encouraged to leave the workplace and return to their roles as homemakers and mothers. The former welders and aircraft workers in *Rosie the Riveter* are clear about what was happening:

> It was a whole different propaganda to let women know what they should be doing. The magazines they start telling you how to cook things that take a long time. Before they were telling you how to cook the dishes you could cook quick and get on to work. Now they were telling you to cook dishes that took a full day.

Many women all over Europe and the United States went back to leading exemplary lives in the kitchen and genuinely enjoyed having their children. Their daughters, by and large, were getting a better deal at school. In Britain the new Education Act of 1944 legally obliged local education authorities to provide primary and secondary education for all children – irrespective of class, race or gender. New grammar schools were set up, many of them giving educational opportunities to girls who passed their state scholarship. It was these girls, like myself, who were to form the next generation of feminists.

Meanwhile, in France, Simone de Beauvoir's *The Second Sex*[9] was published in 1949; blacklisted by the Catholic church, it sent shock waves across Europe – and sold 22,000 copies of the first volume within a week of publication. It was translated and first published in England in 1953. The publication of Betty Friedan's *The Feminine Mystique* in 1965 helped to bring about the re-emergence of the women's movement in North America. Friedan carefully documented the trend for American women to leave the workplace behind in the post-war period from 1945–60 and accept the home and family as their ultimate goal in life. She spoke powerfully to women who had experienced personal growth in the war years and reminded them of their sense of purpose; younger women whose lives were made freer with household appliances began to experience a need to discover themselves:

> The problem lay buried, unspoken, for many years in the minds of American women. It was a strange stirring, a sense of dissatisfaction, a yearning that women suffered in the middle of the twentieth century in the United States. Each suburban housewife struggled with it alone. As she made the beds, shopped for groceries, matched the slipcover material, ate peanut butter sandwiches with her children, chauffeured Cub Scouts and Brownies, lay beside her husband at night, she was afraid to ask even of herself the silent question: 'Is this all?'[10]

By the 1970s women's awareness of inequality had penetrated many areas of life: domesticity, work outside the home, health, child care, media studies and, inevitably, education. In the classroom, feminist researchers uncovered a great deal of inequality in areas like language and gender, the overt and hidden curriculum, the teacher's role, classroom resources, and children's literature. They argued that girls' skills, talents and academic abilities were stunted by the curriculum offered to them and by teaching styles which favoured boys, closing off areas and options to girls which didn't conform to society's expectations of its female citizens.

There was close inspection of the way children talk to their teachers and to each other in single and mixed-sex groups. Their responses to literature were analysed and the subject matter of books and classroom topics received urgent attention. In 1970 Elizabeth Fisher, investigating male and female characters in books written for young children, remarked that:

> Since females comprise 51 per cent of the population of the United States, one would expect them to be equally represented in the world of picture books. On the contrary they vary between 20 and 30 per cent. There were five times as many males in the titles as there were females, four times as many boys, men, or male animals pictures as there were females.[11]

In Britain careful analyses of children's books by Glenys Lobban[12] and Rosemary Stones[13] showed up similar preoccupations with the male presence at the expense of that of girls and women. Stones called for a new kind of writing for children, which portrayed females as lively, complex and interesting characters and which acknowledged women's contribution to history.

At this time, too, appeared Katherine Clarricoates' timely study of the ways in which the hidden and overt curriculum operates in primary schools to the detriment of girls and to the advantage of boys. She documented classroom life and, by so doing, helped teachers to examine their own curricular bias:

> 'Get your books out on dinosaurs please.'
> 'Oh no,' cried the girls. 'Not again, we're always doing boys' topics, Miss.'
> 'Well perhaps later on in the term we'll do something on houses and flowers,' compromises the teacher.
>
> Monosyllabic words and sounds of disgust are emitted from the boys. The children are, by this age, aware of the segregation by

sex in all aspects of classroom life, with boys – and anything connected with them – being looked upon as superior and exciting, whilst girls are treated as inferiors.[14] ✳

Sharply focussed research such as this was given further credibility by the passing of the Sex Discrimination Act in 1975, which made it illegal to discriminate against pupils on the grounds of sex. In the same year the Equal Opportunities Commission was set up by Parliament to monitor the implementation of sex equality, and since then has supported many initiatives and published widely. In 1981 the DES publication *The School Curriculum*[15] showed a clear commitment in government policy towards equal opportunities when it stated: 'It is essential to ensure that equal opportunities are genuinely available to both boys and girls.'

The movement for equal opportunities within education in the last two decades has struggled to improve the position of girls, primarily. Now, though, as our understandings change and grow, there is a significant movement to include the position of boys within the debate. This is important for a variety of reasons, not least because it needs to take account of four-year-old boys like Sean and Terry:

Sean	Get out of it Miss Baxter paxter.
Terry	Get out of it knickers Miss Baxter.
Sean	Get out of it Miss Baxter paxter.
Terry	Get out of it Miss Baxter the knickers paxter knickers, bum.
Sean	Knickers, shit, bum.
Miss B.	Sean, that's enough, you're being silly.
Sean	Miss Baxter, knickers, show your knickers.
Terry	Miss Baxter, show your bum off. (*They giggle.*)
Miss B.	I think you're being very silly.
Terry	Shit Miss Baxter, shit Miss Baxter.
Sean	Miss Baxter, show your knickers your bum off.
Sean	Take all your clothes off, your bra off.
Terry	Yeah, and take your bum off, take your wee-wee off, take your clothes, your mouth off.
Sean	Take your teeth out, take your head off, take your hair off, take your bum off. Miss Baxter the paxter knickers taxter.[16]

The use these small boys make of sexist, violent and oppressive language to position themselves powerfully in relation to their nursery teacher, who has just reprimanded them, needs our urgent attention. The debate, too, needs to embrace the needs and demands of six-year-old Thomas, who interrupts his teacher's explanation of tens and units to explore something that bothers him:

Thomas   Miss, do you love me?
Miss K.   (*Taken aback*) Yes, Thomas, I love you.
Thomas   Do you love me best of all?
Miss K.   Well I think I love my daughter best of all.
Thomas   Are you a mummy?
Miss K.   Yes, Thomas.
Thomas   Teachers can't be mummies.
Miss K.   Yes they can. Lots of teachers are mummies.

And what of David and Clayton, eight-years old, who discuss their reaction to a reading of *Charlotte's Web*[17] like this, and in doing so position themselves in relation to their own feelings and those of the girls:

Julia   Miss it was very sad when Charlotte died. I . . . everyone, nearly everyone cried.
Clayton   Only the boys didn't cry 'cos they were brill.
Boys   Yeah.
David   True Clayton.
Clayton   We don't cry like girls. They're babies.
Boys   True.
Samantha   Miss, I think it's a lump-in-your-throat story 'cos when you're halfway through you have to go (*swallow*) like that.
Karen   Miss I think, erm, why the boys didn't cry is because the girls are more sensitive than boys at stories like that.
Tracy   I think I know why girls sometimes cry 'cos they take things more serious than boys do.
Julia   They don't have feelings.[18]

What should a teacher do when a discussion goes this way in the classroom? How can the teacher help the children to get back in touch with their own feelings and cross the gender divide? Teachers who, ten years ago, might have been concerned only with promoting girls' achievements, now recognise that Thomas, Sean and Terry, David and Clayton live in classrooms alongside girls and female teachers, and need to have their attitudes recognised and, at times, powerfully challenged. The English curriculum needs to offer girls and boys different ways of thinking about their feminine and masculine roles and the expectations they have of themselves and each other as women and men. Perhaps Michelle and Richard, aged nine, reporting on their collaborative survey of girls' and boys' attitudes in their class (Figure 1), offer us a glimpse of a different kind of future.

Simon Like's gril's and he get's along with he play's with gril's he play's chase andfootball with Them Simon Like's Football he say's Grils can Do anything Boy's Can Do witch is right Simon say's gril's are smart But Boy's are not smart so we found a new srot of Boy after all

Figure 1

CHAPTER 2

Learning Gender Roles

How did eight-year-old Karen come to learn that 'girls are more sensitive than boys'? Why does Clayton feel that boys who don't cry are 'brill'? Language, attitudes, expectations, the media, stories – all play their part in reinforcing these gender roles; and the children themselves are not passive recipients of society's messages and images. They actively take part in their own socialisation into masculine and feminine roles through their language, their dress, the choices they make in games, toys and media heroes, the stories they tell about themselves, and their expectations for the future. Social and cultural attitudes about gender are learnt from birth and are modelled and reinforced, often unconsciously, by parents and other significant adults, including teachers. It is possible to track the development of these 'learnt' gender roles from birth onwards to show how they have become firmly established by the time children reach nursery age and are reinforced at school, often by the children themselves, through their use of language and in their play.

In the nursery

In her study of sex-differentiation in nurseries,[19] Julia Hodgeon noted that it was common for the boys to climb, shout, run and jump around while the girls sat by the edge of the play area, perhaps sharing books with an adult. Girls and boys did not generally communicate with each other. On one occasion when some new toys were brought to the nursery the boys took possession of them all, even those which the girls had begun to investigate for themselves. A girl who was hit by a boy complained to a nursery nurse, but she was merely told, 'Oh dear, he is a naughty boy isn't he'; the nursery nurse didn't reprimand the boys. Julia Hodgeon noted that nursery assistants frequently responded to children on the basis of their gender, rather than because of their individual needs and preferences. Girls were told:

'Careful, girls, now you're getting too rough.'
'Come away from the paint, girls. You're going to get it on your clothes.'

When children enter mainstream school in the year they become five, it is hardly surprising that their gender roles are firmly fixed and are part of the way they understand the world and their place within it. Anjuli sees her future as one of care and support (Figure 2) while Christopher projects himself into a vivid fantasy role involving danger and excitement (Figure 3). Andrew's job as a stuntman is combined with a visit to the pub for a pint of beer (Figure 4).

Four- and five-year-old children confirm these futures for themselves in their fantasy play in both classroom and playground. Often the girls in the home corner can be observed practising their future roles as wives and mothers; the boys play at being 'painters and decorators', or 'big bad dogs'. This teacher's observation is by no means unusual:

> On the last day of the summer term the children brought their toys to school. The girls brought their pushchairs, buggies and dolls and played in the home corner. Then they moved their 'home' to a bay outside the classroom and the home corner was taken over by the boys who played Superman, converting the dressing-up clothes into capes and zooming round the classroom. On another occasion a group of boys turned the home corner into a Bat Cave and the chairs and tables became Batmobiles.

The same teacher also noticed that the children in her class played different games at playtime, often in single-sex groups. She discussed this with them and was able to compile these two lists for her class:

What the boys do at playtime	What the girls do at playtime
Teenage Mutant Hero Turtles	skipping
fighting	dancing
monsters	ring-a-roses
Batman	made-up games
football	chasing boys
Superman	talking to friends
wrestling	handstands

In this way the playground becomes a site of meaningful play, where children's games hold powerful metaphors of what it means to be male or female. The boys' games involve team spirit, competitiveness and aggression. They weave games and stories around the vivid imaginative male fantasy worlds they see

Figure 2 I want to be a nurse   *Anjuli (aged five) looks ahead to a life of caring and helping people*

Figure 3 I want to be Batman   *Christopher (aged six) knows Batman from TV and comics and incorporates his hero into his own fantasy life*

In the year 2000 Andrew I will be 17.
In the year 2000 I will have a job
In want to be a stunt man.
and jump off a high building.
and dive on a matress. I will go to
the pub and have a pint to
beer.

Figure 4 When I am 17   *Andrew (aged six) constructs a masculine role for himself as he looks forward to a life of adventure and danger*

on television and in comics, and often have fantasy doll-figures, such as Action Man or Batman, in their play.

The girls play games which often help them to learn to co-operate with each other, and in doing so they learn about relationships – it's interesting that 'talking to friends' features high on their list of activities. They learn skills from each other and from older girls too – clapping and skipping games, dancing, handstands; skills that call for agility and a sense of rhythm. Perhaps their game of 'chasing boys' is an early indication that these girls are a little resentful of the power and privilege of the boys on the playground. The girls' space is frequently invaded by the boys, and the girls complain to their teacher about the way the boys break up their games by interfering, by kicking the football across their skipping line, or by charging wildly through their dancing space.

As these children become part of the new community of the school they experience growing peer-group pressure from their own sex to conform to gender-roles. This conversation between five-year-old Selena and her mother shows the pressure Selena puts on herself to behave like a 'little girl':

Mum	What about toys for Christmas? Selena, shall I get you a truck?
Selena	Yes, but not for outside.
Mum	Not for outside. Why not?
Selena	'Cos girls will see me.
Mum	Girls will see you? Why not? What's wrong with that? You mean the girls will laugh at you because you had a truck for Christmas?
Selena	Yes.

Like many of the girls in her class, Selena owns a Sindy Doll, a doll presented to girls as a sexual woman for them to dress in fashionable style. Evidence that they already model themselves in her constraining image is given by Selena's teacher, who says:

> The image of the Sindy Doll is often transferred to the clothes that some small girls wear. Often their clothing is impractical, inhibiting their movements. They wear shoes they can't run in properly, and which deny them the opportunity of joining in the more physical games they would enjoy.

Dolls for the boys are an extension of their fantasy play and take the form of Action Men, Action Force men, Transformers, or models of Teenage Mutant Hero Turtles, Batman or Superman. They present the boys with images of themselves in their male fantasy worlds, acting on the universe in a way which makes them feel powerful and dangerous.

The children use their own developing language to travel into their fantasy worlds. Seven-year-old Duane told this story to his teacher after he'd watched the film of *Jaws III*:

Figure 5

Well he bit off his arm. Well there was this tunnel under the water. And he went and with his hand on his back he bashed it and all the people fell into the water and then he didn't bother about them but he went to this ground under water. All these people are doing writing and when they were writing Jaws came. A white man and a black man saw them. He bashed the glass and one man got air and then they went out and then this woman went in the water right and Jaws was down. He was only a little baby then, right, but when the woman went in he was a big fully shark and then Jaws went and bit her leg and it was all bleeding but it never came off and then they catched the shark but it wasn't Jaws, no. They catched another shark. It was Jaws but they weren't sure so they saw one of the people what was on the beach so er it was Jaws and so they killed him.

Duane uses these fantasies of power and domination to act out the masculine role that, as a boy, he must strive for. Robert, also aged seven, has a fantasy world filled with images and stories of monsters of one kind and another, like the powerful three-headed dinosaur-like creature he draws here (Figure 6). He often invents frightening and dangerous dramas, and in this story he and the other boy he writes about (but perhaps significantly does not draw), control the monster by gently leading it home.

Figure 6

— 18 —

Many girls of this age are busy writing about domestic events as they begin to position themselves in the feminine role of homemaker and carer: their families, friends and pets – vital relationships in their lives – feature largely in their fantasies. Sharon was seven when she wrote this safe, comfortable story of friendship and support:

> One day a little rabbit said to a bird do you want dinner with me and the bird said I will go and see the swan and the swan said yes. Come with me and the swan went with the bird. The swan and the bird said the dinner was nice.

But while there is an acceptance of this feminine role on the part of many of the girls, there is also resentment for some, and the growing need to shape their lives by telling a different story of their futures. Hayley, aged seven, frames her future with a story she tells about herself. But could she be helped to tell a different story?

> Well I don't really want to, but I expect I will have a baby and go and visit my friends and go up the pub. I don't want a baby especially if it's a boy 'cos they're a pain. My mum's got a baby and I'm always having to clean up after him.

This tension does not go away for girls. Apwinder, aged ten, tells this story of her future:

> I'd like to be a secretary or a journalist. I'd like to go round the world asking for things, getting my name in the papers, things like that. I'd like to go to America, Australia and Russia. I think I'll get married at 20 or 21. I'd like my mum to look after my baby or my sister. I wouldn't want to get a babysitter.

By this age the girls have entered a world where their female group identity is of great importance to them. And the playground games and rhymes which have formed part of their experience since they started school bond these girls together and help them to explore the difficult area of growing up female. Here is one skipping rhyme, sung in playgrounds in the Midlands:

> Not last night but the night before
> Twenty-four robbers came knocking at the door
> As I went out to let them in . . .
> This is what they said to me
>
> Spanish lady turn around
> Spanish lady touch the ground

Spanish lady do high kicks
Spanish lady show your knicks.

Slightly risqué, and the property of girls only, this rhyme is part
of an oral tradition kept alive and handed down by these girls to
smaller girls in the playground. Other rhymes are a way of
collectively challenging the power of boys:

My friend Billy had a ten foot willy
show it to the girl next door
thought it was a snake
and hit it with a rake
and now it's only four foot four[20]

Rhymes and games like this don't form part of the classroom
curriculum and, by and large, girls are intensely wary of singing
them for performance, and rightly so, for they are embedded in
their play rituals, and form part of their private world. Some of
the rhymes explore important themes – being born, getting
married, becoming a mother, growing old and dying. The words
of these rhymes will vary from playground to playground and up
and down the country, but the subject matter remains constant.
A group of ten-year-old girls play this version of 'Suzie' in
Coventry:

When Suzie was a baby
A baby Suzie was.
She went a-ga, ga, a-ga, ga, ga.

When Suzie was at playgroup
At playgroup Suzie was.
She went a-play, play, a-play, play, play.

When Suzie was an infant
An infant Suzie was.
She went a-scribble, scribble, a-scribble, scribble, scribble.

When Suzie was a junior
A junior Suzie was.
She went a-write, write, a-write, write, write.

When Suzie was a second year
A second year Suzie was.
She went a-miss, miss, I can't do this,
I've got my knickers in a jumble twist.

When Suzie was a teenager
A teenager Suzie was.

She went a-ha, ah, I lost my bra,
I lost my knickers in my boyfriend's car.

When Suzie was a mother
A mother Suzie was.
She went a-wash, scrub, a-rub, rub, rub.

When Suzie was a granny,
A granny Suzie was.
She went a-knit, knit, a-knit, knit, knit.

When Suzie was a skeleton,
A skeleton Suzie was.
She went a-ooh, ooh, a-ooh, ooh, ooh.

It is possible to view the subject matter and the girls' obvious enjoyment of songs like 'Suzie' as a clear reflection of an oppressive stereotype of female life from birth to death, which the girls largely accept. But it is also possible to see within it a female cultural form and a celebration of self through an intensely private and personal language known only to girls. There are ways, perhaps, of conveying this knowledge to the children themselves.

As teachers we need to think beyond these feminine and masculine stereotypes towards ways of promoting equality in our schools which take into account the social, political and cultural implications of what it means to become 'gendered' in our society. We can begin to do this within our own classrooms by paying attention to the language and learning we promote through our English curriculum.

CHAPTER 3

Taking Action in the Classroom: A Climate for Learning

▬ Collaborative enterprise ▬

The classroom practice outlined in this chapter is based on, or has grown out of, collaborative enterprise within the classroom. This is not accidental. Gender is part of a broader issue of democracy in the classroom: negotiating learning, respecting our own and each other's knowledge and opinions, and managing the classroom to ensure that this happens. When girls and boys are encouraged to co-operate by exploring ideas and feelings, by listening to each other, and by asking questions and negotiating meanings in an atmosphere of trust and support, then they are much more likely to value and respect each other's judgements and points of view. There is plenty of evidence to show that children learn best when they work together like this, gaining experience and confidence through talking, listening, reading and writing with different people in different settings.

Children's talking and learning in the classroom is affected by the social context in which it takes place, so the climate needs to be one that invites and plans for children to co-operate and enjoy the freedom to express themselves. When ten-year-old James wrote a successful story his teacher suggested that he should try to talk on tape with another boy, Steven, about how he'd written it. Other people could then learn from his experience and he had an opportunity of making the process of writing explicit for himself. This is an extract from the tape James and Steven made together:

Steven   What was it like when you done your story?
James   It was er well it was all right. It was easy. Very easy indeed.
Steven   How long was your story?
James   About ten minutes say.
Steven   Have you read it to anyone yet, your story?
James   The teacher's read it to our class yes, but that's all. Oh and I've read it to my mum and my brother.
Steven   Have you read it to any infants?
James   No not yet, but I think I might be able to one day.
Steven   Will you read it to your friend Paul in Class 8?

James	Yeah and I might go round the classes and read it to each class 'cos it's only about five . . . ten minutes.
Steven	Will you give a photocopy to every class?
James	If I have enough, yes, probably will. And it will be my greatest hit.
Steven	Would you read it in assembly?
James	Yeah, I could do it in the Friday assembly because the whole school would be there, but even so if I'm giving a copy to each class it would be stupid because they would have, the teacher would probably er do it then . . .
Steven	But you could give it before you give it to the one class. In assembly you could give them to the teachers.
James	Yeah I could go round and ask if she's read it and then give it to each other. It's a good idea Steven. Round of applause for Steven everyone.

James' teacher is particularly aware of the need for these boys to work together in a way which helps them to avoid the masculine constraints of competitiveness which they so often impose on themselves. In this way their collaboration can become part of an anti-sexist process. The boys reflect on James' story and the format he chose for it. They make sense of his experience, and re-create it, and then Steven helps James to decide how he will make the story available throughout the school. Much of this talk is business-like and practical as they plan what will happen to the story. Parts of James' talk are celebratory: after all, he's written a good story – and Steven helps him to give it significance. They're talking about something that's very real to them and so they talk with a sense of purpose. There's a vital human dimension to their talk too: it's about living, about the textures of school life, and a common concern. Steven supports his friend by setting the framework for discussion and asking some searching questions which help James to move his planning forward.

In spite of this, James and Steven demonstrate through their language just how powerful the masculine constraints of competitiveness are for them, and even though there is a general willingness to conform to their teacher's alternative culture, there are strong echoes of male-gendered identity in the way they handle the situation, with James often playing the hero-role and Steven posing some threatening questions. In this respect, the tape they made has the feel of a performance, with an underlying edge of competitiveness, and where both boys often lack the courage to be vulnerable and tentative. James' final utterance confirms this.

Nevertheless, James and Steven know that their teacher respects their opinions and will trust them to find out for themselves what they can make their language do, and how they can make it serve their own purposes by using it to plan something that will form a focus for James' work on the following day. The organisational role of the teacher is crucial in making space for James and Steven to take control of their own learning like this. Their classroom is a place where co-operation is valued and space is made for children to listen to one another's ideas and, in this instance, to use their talk to come to a better understanding of sharing writing with younger audiences. The boys know too that it's appropriate for their talk to be speculative and hesistant – even if they can't as yet admit to this publicly – and that this kind of talk will enable them to think ahead about what they want to say and do next.

Programmes of Study for the National Curriculum

Collaborative learning is advocated in many of the activities outlined in the Programmes of Study.

Speaking and Listening

Key Stage 1   The range of activities should include:

● discussion of their work with other pupils and the teacher.

Key Stage 2   The range of opportunities provided should:

● allow pupils to work in groups of various sizes, both single sex and mixed where possible, with and without direct teacher supervision.

Reading

Key Stage 1   Activities should ensure that pupils:

● talk to the teacher and each other about the books and stories they have been reading or listening to.

Key Stage 2   Pupils should:

● keep records of their own reading and comment, in writing or in discussion, on the books which they have read.

Writing

Key Stage 1

● pupils should write individually and in groups, sharing their writing with others and discussing what they have written.

Key Stage 2   Pupils should:

● have opportunities to write poetry (individually, in small groups or as a class).

Raising children's awareness in the classroom

Raising children's awareness of gender issues and of themselves as gendered beings is a key part of the process of helping them to regulate their behaviour in socially responsible ways that enhance their potential for learning. The democratic English curriculum is about making this happen in each of the language modes – speaking, listening, reading and writing, and in learning about language itself. Classroom activities, if presented carefully, can help children to move beyond their own potentially damaging, stereotyped behaviour into new ways of thinking and being.

Unlikely situations

Children can be helped towards an understanding of how they take on gender roles if they are confronted by unusual or opposite situations which enable them to make comparisons and to think through new possibilities. One way of doing this is to use pictures or photographs that you have re-jigged in order to show women and men, boys and girls doing things that are usually considered more appropriate for the other sex, for example:

- a boy playing with a Sindy doll
- a man cleaning the lavatory
- a girl playing with a remote control car
- a man knitting
- a woman emptying dustbins.

The surprise is usually so great that you should find no difficulty in getting the children to talk about the images you have provided.

1 In same-sex pairs, do a survey in your school of children and adults who play or work in ways that seem unusual for someone of their sex. Talk to them about what they are doing and why. Report your findings to your class.

2 Write letters of invitation to adults in your community who are doing jobs which seem unusual for someone of their sex. Ask them to come into school to talk to your class about their work and why they chose to do it. (The Equal Opportunities Commission might be able to help you to get in touch with suitable people, if you don't know any. Their address is Overseas House, Quay Street, Manchester M3 3HN.)

3 In mixed-sex groups do a survey in your school to find out what everybody's favourite toy is. Put your results on to a chart. It might look like this:

Class 1 Age: 6-7	Toy	Boy	Girl
Darren	gun	✓	
Harrinder	jigsaw		✓
Susan	doll		✓
Raj	Action Man	✓	

Report your findings to everyone in a school assembly.

Tasks for children: *unlikely situations*

Making observations

Two ten-year-old girls made these observations in note form of four and five year olds in the home corner:

> Two girls and one boy in wendy house. Girls are tidying up while boy comes in and looks after the baby. Charlene makes tea. Emma tidies out the cupboard. Raj pretends to fix roof and phones police then goes shopping.

They had been asked to make observations of different groups of children in the school as they worked and played. The point was not to make judgements about what the children were doing, but merely to report on what they had seen.

This activity was designed to help children begin to look in a new way at so-called normal everyday behaviour, to see if there are patterns within it and to look at ways of relating it to themselves and their own lives. The same idea can be applied in a number of different ways. Children might be asked to observe:

- a girl and boy in a nursery or playgroup
- a girl and boy in a class of five year olds
- a girl and boy in a class of eight year olds
- a girl and boy at playtime
- a girl and boy at dinnertime.

Work in mixed-sex pairs to observe and record children at work and at play in your school. You will need to write quickly in note form. Alternatively, you could record your observations into a tape recorder and write up your findings later.

Report back to your class and discuss what you found. You will need to present your findings clearly so that everyone understands them. Think carefully about how you want to do this. One way would be to make a chart which you could show on the overhead projector screen. It might look like this:

Location: playground	Number of children observed	Sex	Age	comment
	2	boys	5	playing Batman
	6 1	girls boy	6	skipping together.
	1	boy	7	Standing on his own by the wall

Tasks for children: *making observations*

What do other people think?

Questionnaires offer a way for children to discover and explore other people's attitudes and opinions. One class of ten year olds planned a general questionnaire for children of their own age and asked for responses to a number of provocative statements about gender-stereotyping:

- boys are stronger than girls
- girls are more intelligent than boys
- men never cry
- boys don't play with dolls
- girls are not as brave as boys
- women should try to look beautiful all the time
- men are useless at looking after babies
- girls shouldn't swear.

Other groups might prefer a more conventional style of question:

- What is your favourite sport?
- When you leave school what kind of work would you like to do?
- What occupations do you feel are only done by women?
- What occupations do you feel are only done by men?
- Why did you choose to do the job you're doing?
- Do you think your job would be done better by a person of the opposite sex?

As well as helping to raise children's awareness of gender-stereotyping by examining other people's views, this activity will also help children to plan and work together, and give them experience of writing for a wider readership.

In mixed-sex groups design and write your own questionnaire. You will need to think carefully about:

- what it is you want to find out.
- how you will write your questions or statements so that whoever reads your questionnaire will know exactly what you mean.
- who your questionnaire is for. (It might be for children in your own class, children in another class, your parents, your teachers, your school governors, your cooks, your cleaners, your caretaker . . . and so on.)

Think of ideas for your questionnaire and write these down in note form. Report back to the whole class about the content of your group's questionnaire. Have you covered all the important areas? If not, decide how you can do this.

Now design and write your questionnaire. (Think how many languages you need to write it in.) Check spelling and punctuation.

Decide how many copies you need and then duplicate your questionnaire.

Write a note to go out with your questionnaire explaining what you are doing and why it would be helpful for you to receive a completed questionnaire. Thank people in advance for taking the time to fill it in. Make sure they know where to return the questionnaires (e.g. Please return to: Red group, Mrs Slater's class, Elmtree School, Green Road, Birmingham).

When your questionnaires have been returned, analyse the responses in your groups and share the information with your class. Write to the people who filled them in, and tell them what you found out.

Tasks for children: *what do other people think?*

Exploring your own attitudes

Children need time to explore their own feelings about their gender identity through both talking and writing. Here is Louise, for example, writing about the differences between boys and girls:

about boys and girls

I think boys are messier than girls because they get holes in there jumpers and trousers and there shirts and girls never get holes in there clothes and boys are messier than girls because boys s push other boys over but girls play nicely but boys dont but boys think they are ace because they think that they can do every think but they cant because the cant do a head stand or a bridge so they can not do ever--y think

by louise

Figure 7

Samantha and Dawn, on the other hand, are preoccupied with what it means to be a 'tomboy':

you have to have a brother Before you can be a tomboy because you will know what to do. I've got two brother's and I go with them when they play out and I play foot ball and I climb trees. I go butter fly catching. I do lot's of thing like Boys.

Dawn

A Tom boy is Someone how has
a bROTHER my friends a tom boy
but I Dont think She is because
SHe has not got a bRother
So she is not atom boy
Samantha

Figure 8

Other starting points might include asking children:

- how their parents and grandparents treat them differently from their brothers, or sisters
- if their brothers, or sisters, have different interests, and why this might be.

---

1 In single-sex groups, discuss some of the issues you have been talking about as a whole class: tomboys, brothers and sisters, the way you're treated differently by parents and grandparents. Make notes about the things you say.

2 By yourself, write about something you feel strongly about to do with being a girl or boy. It can be private or you could share it with your teacher, your group or your class.

Tasks for children: *exploring your own attitudes*

Programmes of Study for the National Curriculum

Programmes of Study that are covered by these activities:

Speaking and listening

Key Stage 1   The range of activities should include:

- securing responses to visual stimuli e.g. pictures.

Key Stage 2   Pupils should be given the opportunity to learn how to:

- express and justify feelings, opinions and viewpoints with increasing sophistication.
- present factual material in a clear logically structured manner in a widening range of situations.

Reading

Key Stage 1 Activities should ensure that pupils:

- make their own books about particular experiences.

Key Stage 2 Pupils should:

- be shown how to read different kinds of materials in different ways.

Writing

Key Stage 1 Pupils should:

- write individually and in groups, sharing their writing with others and discussing what they have written.
- undertake a range of chronological writing including . . . personal experiences.

Key Stage 2 Pupils should:

- write personal letters to known recipients and be shown how to set them out.
- be helped to understand that non-chronological types of writing can be organised in a variety of ways and so, generally, require careful planning; this might include the presentation of information.

▬ *Learning about language* ▬

The way language is used in society is a reflection of our cultural values and the way we think about things and people. It carries messages about our worth, the power we hold or do not hold, our position in relation to the other sex, to people older and younger than ourselves and to those in different ethnic groups.

The 'Knowledge about Language' strand within the National Curriculum for English gives enormous scope for investigating this important area. Children are expected to have started work on learning about language 'by the time [they] are working towards level 5'. Even so, younger children's knowledge and understanding of language is extensive, and Programmes of Study intended for children working between Key Stage 2 and 4 can be interpreted appropriately for younger children.

You might, for example, discuss with them the ways in which boys and girls talk and write from early childhood onwards. Their awareness of differences in language use, and the possible reasons for this, should develop as they begin to interpret and reflect on the evidence they collect in such activities as those that follow.

Baby talk

1 Some people have noticed that children and grown-ups talk to babies differently, depending on whether the baby is a girl or a boy.
   - How would you talk to a baby girl?
   - How would you talk to a baby boy?
   - Would you talk to baby boys and girls in different ways? If so, why should this be?
   - How would you talk to a baby if you didn't know the sex of the child?

Discuss this in mixed-sex groups.

2 If you have a baby at home, listen to the way grown-ups talk to him or her. Or visit your parent and toddler group at school and listen to the ways mothers and fathers there talk to young children. Are there any differences in the way the grown-ups talk to little boys and the way they talk to little girls? Make notes about this and report back to your class.

3 Make a collection of congratulation cards that are sent to mothers and fathers when their babies are born – or bring your own into school if you still have them. Study them carefully to see if there is a difference between the kinds of things they say about baby boys and what they say about baby girls. Make notes about this and report back to your class.

Tasks for children: *learning about language (1)*

Observing little children

1 In mixed-sex pairs, watch small children in the nursery or playgroup at school, or in their first-year class, and listen carefully to the way they talk:
   - in the home corner
   - to their teacher
   - to their friends
   - to someone they fall out with.

Are there any differences in the way boys and girls talk? What are these differences? Make careful notes.

2 Listen carefully to the children's teachers. Do they seem to be talking differently to boys and girls? Once again, make careful notes. Talk to the teachers afterwards about the things you've found out.

3 Watch how little children play with their toys and notice if there are any differences in the kinds of things children say when they are

playing with:

- a doll
- a train
- lego.

Find out if different toys help little children to use language in different ways. Is there a way of talking that's only for the girls and a way of talking that's only for the boys? If so, is this a good thing?

4 In mixed-sex groups, role-play arguments between:

- two girls
- two boys
- a girl and a boy.

Were they different? If so, in what way? Why do you think this was?

Now, replay the same arguments with:

- two boys arguing as if they were two girls
- two girls arguing as if they were two boys.

What did you notice? How did it feel to be part of that argument? Did anyone use language in a different way?

Tasks for children: *learning about language (2)*

How much do *you* talk?

Some people listened to boys and girls talking in classrooms and they noticed that the boys spent much more time talking than the girls did, and that the teacher had to spend more time listening to the boys than to the girls. Is this the case in your classroom? See if you can find out.

During a class discussion time listen carefully to who is talking and record your information. You could make a chart like this:

Boy asks a question	///
Boy interrupts	////
Girl asks a question	/
Girl interrupts	
Teacher responds to boy	//
Teacher responds to girl	/

Share what you've found out with your teacher and class. If you discover that boys are talking more than girls, what can you do about it?

Tasks for children: *learning about language (3)*

Programmes of Study for the National Curriculum

Programmes of Study that are covered in these activities of 'Learning about language':

Speaking and listening

Key Stage 1   The range of activities should include:

● collaborative planning of activities in a way which requires pupils to speak and listen.

Key Stage 2   The range of activities should include:

● the preparation of presentations.

With particular reference to Knowledge about language:

Key Stages 2 to 4   Teaching about language through speaking and listening . . . should focus on:

● the range of purposes which spoken language serves
● the forms and functions of spoken Standard English.

Reading

Key Stage 1   Activities should ensure that pupils:

● talk about the content of information texts.

Key Stage 2   Pupils should:

● be shown how to read different kinds of materials in different ways.

Writing

Key Stage 1   Pupils should:

● undertake a range of non-chronological writing.

Key Stage 2   Pupils should:

● use writing to learn and record their experiences.

CHAPTER 4

Taking Action in the Classroom: Working Together for Change

▬ Different roles: possible futures ▬

Educational researchers have made the point forcibly over the last few years that our dedication to 'free choice' and 'free activity' in the early years of schooling can constrain both girls and boys, because even at this early age children tend to choose classroom activities that support gender roles learnt through interaction with their family, community and the media; consequently they are not free to choose, because they often restrict themselves to the kinds of activities with which they feel secure[21]. Early-years teachers are recognising that they need to intervene in children's play to ensure that they experience equal opportunities through a broad range of activities.

markmaking
writing area
home corner
construction corner

Making changes in the Wendy House

One particular initiative has been to change the nature of children's role-play in the 'home corner'.

It is important to consider why it might be necessary to make changes around what, after all, has been a standard item of play furniture in young children's classrooms for a great many years, enabling them to involve themselves in a great deal of imaginative play and language. Furthermore, it can be said that this is perhaps one area where girls exert a powerful influence, since they often seem to be fully in control of the play situations they generate. This is a conversation between two four year olds in their home corner:

Sherine   Come on, Mum.
Geeta   I'm not Mum. We're two sisters.
Sherine   You hold the dog. I'll have the baby. (*She gets a doll out of the box for herself and a toy dog for Geeta.*)
Geeta   We both have babies. (*She reaches in the box for another doll.*) This is my baby and I'll have the dog too. I'm going to the park.[22]

These two girls use their language and their firm grasp of narrative to support each other in creating a powerful make-believe world, where Geeta is so much in control that she can embrace the roles of both mother and sister. The girls also rehearse a possible adult future for themselves as they examine their relationships and their place within the family. These stories girls invent for themselves are powerful and necessary – and we can help them to extend them, to begin to tell other stories of possible futures for themselves.[23]

One infant teacher became disturbed by the sameness of the girls' play she witnessed daily in the home corner (she had already changed the name from Wendy House, with its feminine connotations). She was also deeply concerned about the behaviour of the small boys who frequently disrupted life in the home corner by playing 'big, bad dogs', 'painters and decorators' and 'robbers'. Did they do it because they were unable to find a dominant role for themselves since the girls appeared to be in control of the situations they created? Or was it to do with the necessity of acting out the roles offered to them in media narratives, the heroes from the fantasy worlds of TV and comics? She wondered how to help the boys to invent and enter positive new fictional worlds that were equally creative but perhaps broader and less limiting.

She talked to her class about the possibility of converting the home corner into a café, with cooks, waiters and waitresses, customers, and a telephone service for booking tables and ordering meals. The children responded well and though the café was painted, robbed and on one occasion overrun by big, bad dogs, the role-play was quite successful, though the teacher noted that the girls found it easier to step into new roles than the boys did. The home corner then became a medical centre with doctors, nurses, patients and clerical support. Once again, the girls were better organised, but the boys did begin to take on caring roles within the organisation. The corner has since been an office and is now a railway station, complete with train, ticket office (with tickets, money, timetables, and telephone) and children take it in turn to be guards, drivers, clerks and passengers.

These role-play situations have given the children new experiences. The girl engine driver, in her luminous orange top, is fully in charge of the situation: 'Get on the train everyone. Tell me where to drive. We're going to London!' she announces as she sits confidently in the front of the train, pretending to drive, in charge of both the machine and the people. The boys have creative roles that have built-in constraints on their behaviour: if they are drivers they have to wait patiently while the passengers come aboard; if they are guards, they have to wait until everything is ready before they blow their whistle. In other words, they are obliged to act responsibly in a situation where they have to take account of other people. Turn-taking and sharing is encouraged by this kind of role-play, where the children have been offered a new set of roles, each with their own rules, and encouraged to look towards new horizons, different futures and new relationships with themselves and others.

Intervening in construction tasks

In the same school,[24] teachers noticed that the girls were on the whole not enthusiastic about making use of construction materials; boys were, but tended to make only guns, cars and so on. The teachers decided that intervention was necessary to help both the girls and boys play with construction equipment in new ways. The classes of Year 2 and Year 3 children were grouped in threes and each group contained two girls and one boy, wherever possible, to support the girls in a new activity they were unsure about, and to ensure that the boys played a less dominant role. Their teachers devised ideas for the children with three major principles: girls and boys would be required to co-operate with each other; the tasks should not alienate the girls from dealing with construction toys; the tasks would provide alternative views of gender roles. The tasks were written on cards and placed on the table with appropriate construction materials. They were:

- My grass needs cutting. Make a machine to do it for me, please.
- Can you make a machine that will help you with your writing?
- The playground needs some interesting apparatus. Make swings, slides and other things.
- We need a machine that makes sweets.
- I have fallen down and broken my leg. Please make me a wheelchair.
- Make a machine that will cut your hair.
- Make a machine for cooking food.
- Can you make a house for your pet dog?
- Let's make some furniture for the house.
- Can you make something to help my baby sleep?

As the children carried out the tasks the teachers discussed ideas with them and helped them to develop their plans.

New roles in the family

The teachers also intervened in the children's imaginative construction play by providing a series of task cards with different situations for them to represent and enact. They were:

- Dad is a nurse in a hospital. He helps everybody get better.
- Aunty goes to work. Uncle goes to the shops with the children.
- Mum goes to work. Dad and the children get a meal ready.
- Some people are coming to visit. Dad and the children make a party for them.
- Make a farm. The farmer drives the tractor. She feeds all the animals.
- Big sister drives the milk lorry. She takes the milk to all the houses.
- Mum drives a fire engine. She puts out all the fires.
- Mum's job is being a doctor. She goes to see people when they are ill.
- Everything in the house breaks down. Mum fixes all the machines.
- The family goes on a picnic. Dad gets the food ready. Mum drives the car. The car breaks down. Mum fixes it.
- Two sisters, a brother and a baby are in the garden. The brother looks after the baby. The two sisters play.
- Mum goes to work. Dad takes the children to the park.

Evidence that some of the children are tentatively trying out new roles for themselves, aided by the intervention of a teacher, is provided in this transcript of a group activity where three children (two girls and a boy) are working with the task card: 'Mum goes out to work. Dad takes the children to the park'. Using Lego, the children had first made a house and an office. They were then given a toy car and little wooden dolls:

Mum	OK. Let's have breakfast. (*To child*) What do you want?
Teacher	Don't forget you have to go to work. Dad can make breakfast.
Dad	But I've been working all night. I've just come back.
Teacher	No, you haven't got a job outside. Your wife works in an office. You can stay at home.
Dad	OK then. Let me make breakfast.
Mum	All right – bye-bye. Kiss, kiss (*to child*). Bye dear. Oh . . . what do you want me to buy from the shops?
Teacher	Why not let Dad do the shopping? You go to the office.
Mum	Right. Bye-bye. (*Takes car to office.*)

Dad	(*To child*) What do you want for breakfast?
Child	Cornflakes . . . tea . . . and eggs.
Dad	OK. Here's your breakfast. Let's go to the park.
Teacher	Wait. Aren't you going to get dressed?
Dad	Oh . . . OK . . . Must get the car. (*Reaches out to take car from office front.*)
Teacher	But your wife has got the car.
Dad	Yeah . . . but we need it to go to the park.
Teacher	But can't you walk to the park?
Dad	(*Groans*) But we want the car.
Teacher	But your wife needs it at work.
Dad	All right . . . let's go . . . (*pause*)
Teacher	(*To Dad*) What are you going to do now?
Dad	I don't know.
Child	Hmmm . . . we'll go shopping.
Teacher	Take the bus.
Dad	(*Thinks*) . . . We'll walk . . .
Dad	(*In the shop: to child*) What do you want?
Child	Sweets, chocolate.
Dad	OK. Here you are.
Teacher	But are they good for your teeth?
Dad	No . . . (*to child*) What do you want?
Child	Adidas shoes . . .
Mum	Ooh . . . They're spending all my money!
Dad	But it's my money. I go to work at night.
Teacher	Never mind . . . never mind . . . let's go home now.
Mum	All right . . . I'm home dear . . . Oh . . . Let me get out of my coat . . . and scarf and gloves. All right what do you want for dinner . . . ?

In this extract the children are made to look at different possibilities for themselves in the role-play that has been set up for them and by the timely intervention of the teacher, who pushes Dad into a new acceptance of his role as house-husband, and Mum into her new role as breadwinner.

Programmes of Study for the National Curriculum

In these role-play situations young children have used their language in a variety of ways:

- to enter the world of their imagination through role-play
- to write and read notices, timetables, menus, tickets and so on, in the café, office and railway station
- to read instruction cards.

They are fulfilling these Programmes of Study for *Key Stage 1*:

Speaking and listening

The range of activities should include:

- collaborative and exploratory play
- giving and receiving simple explanations, information and instructions; asking and answering questions.

Reading

Activities should ensure that pupils:

- read in the context of role-play and dramatic play *e.g. in the home, play corner, class shop or other dramatic play setting such as a café, hospital or post office.*

Writing

Pupils should:

- undertake a range of non-chronological writing which includes . . . lists, labels, notices, posters.

▬ *Children and their reading* ▬

The APU Primary Language Survey[25] made several important findings that relate to gender-roles in the primary school. They are that, on the whole:

- Girls read more quickly than boys.
- Girls prefer to read fiction.
- Boys prefer to read information books.
- Girls prefer creative poetry and letter writing.
- Boys prefer factual writing and see fewer purposes for writing than girls.

These findings can have important implications for gender equality and the development of language experiences for girls and boys in the primary years. Children need to experience a wide range of reading material and experiment with many styles of writing. Where necessary, boys need to be encouraged to read fiction and girls to read non-fiction. Teachers can help here by being good reading models themselves; if it's possible, boys and girls should see male teachers in their school reading and enjoying fiction, perhaps at quiet reading time, at storytime, and reading and telling stories in assemblies. And those girls who are avid readers need encouragement to read even more challenging books – it is too easy to allow them to read in an unsupervised fashion, since they appear to be succeeding anyway.

Children's books: looking at gender

There have been many research studies in this important area in the last twenty years. Reading schemes, picture-story books, novels for older readers, folk and fairy tales and non-fiction texts have all come under the close scrutiny of teachers and researchers anxious to offer children the kind of stories that reflect positive images of girls and boys, men and women. Researchers have made major points about many of the books that line the shelves of our primary schools, and these can be summarised as follows:

- Women and men, girls and boys are often portrayed, in both text and illustration, in stereotyped and limiting roles.
- Sexist language is a common feature of the writing.
- Heroes greatly outnumber heroines.
- Male writers outnumber female writers.

It matters that we take note of books that can be described like this, because if they are in our schools then they are part of our curriculum, whether we want them to be or not, and they inevitably become part of the cultural patterning of the children's lives: the stories they read and the stories they tell about themselves become enmeshed.

We need books for children that don't dodge the important issues: books about being born, growing up and dying[26]; stories about the danger, struggle and challenge of growing towards independence; stories about the emotions that accompany us on our journey through life: anger, fear, guilt, joy. We also need to introduce children to authors and illustrators who know about the conflicts of growing towards maturity. And we need to seek out authors who are able to show children that the courage, intelligence, compassion, humour, and friendship they will need throughout their lives are qualities that can be found in both sexes. Fortunately there are plenty of authors and illustrators producing good fiction for children, and the choice for teachers has probably never been greater (see Resources, pp. 73–75).

Exploring gender issues in children's books

It is possible to involve even young children in the debate about choice and quality of books in the classroom. Raising their awareness of the issues can be a powerful way of helping them to learn how books come to be written in the way they are. David, Sharon, Nicola and Grant, all aged eight, became interested in this area. They chose one hundred fiction books from their shelves and counted the heroes and heroines in the stories. This was the result of their survey, which David wrote up and the group presented to their class:

We have done a survey on 100 Books
to find out about how many
female heroes there were in different
Books and this is what we found
62 male heroes and there were
26 female heroes and there were
12 of both there were more
males then females.

Figure 9

A survey of this kind provides an opportunity for classroom
discussion about possible reasons why there are so many male
and so few female characters in children's stories.

In groups, devise your own checklist for surveying books in your
classroom. Divide your story books equally between the groups. Your
checklist could look like this:

Title	
Author	
Publisher	
Year published	
Main character(s) male/female/both	
Girls in the story are brave, intelligent, kind, sensible. YES/NO	
Boys in the story are brave, intelligent, kind, sensible. YES/NO	

Girls in the story are silly, helpless, not very clever, cowardly. YES/NO	
Boys in the story are silly, helpless, not very clever, cowardly. YES/NO	
Any other comments	

Collect the results of your survey and publish them for your class. What kinds of things do you notice? What can you do about it?

Tasks for children: *exploring gender in books*

Exploring the issues further

Teachers who use literature to raise gender issues will almost certainly meet deeply ingrained attitudes on the part of some of the children and must be ready to deal with conflict positively so that the children don't feel threatened and are able to move their thinking forward. A class discussion about *Charlotte's Web* revealed deeply-held beliefs about gender roles in these eight year olds:[27]

Teacher	The story was written by E.B. White. Samantha and Natasha and David said 'she' when we talked about the author, and Clayton said he thought he was probably a man.
Clayton	'Cos it's more like a man's story. Men don't cry when . . . spiders die. Women do, they're so stupid.
Samantha	Miss it's like when you go to the wedding. I didn't know whether to cry or laugh. It's like that in some stories as well.
Clayton	It's not a lady's story. It's not a lady's story.
Teacher	What's a lady's story Clayton?
Clayton	Well you wouldn't get a woman writing about a pig would you?
Karen	Miss and I know why that is.
Nathan	They smell.
Karen	'Cos ladies don't like pigs as much as men, 'cos boys are pigs.

This kind of discussion is not unusual: teachers need to be prepared for it to surface and find ways of exploring ideas and feelings with their own class so that the group feels positively about what they have achieved.

Picture-story books can be used with early-years children to raise debates about gender roles. One teacher read *Piggybook*[28] by Anthony Browne to her class of five and six year olds. In this book the mother of the family services her husband and two sons: cooking, setting the table, serving food, clearing up, and so on. Gradually all the objects in the house turn into pigs – the roses on the wallpaper, even the teapot and, of course, the father and both the sons: one enormous metaphor visually displayed – and mother leaves home. Only then do the boys make their beds while father does the ironing. Mother returns, and mends the car. The pigs disappear. The children in this class discuss the story with their teacher, who intervenes to take the children's thinking forward and build on remarks they make:

Sundip	(*Looking at the illustration of mother mending the car*) She could hoover inside but she can't do that, fix it.
Lisa	Yes she can. Ladies can do it sometimes, they can. They learn how to do it.
Johnny	Ladies can't fix cars. They don't know what to do.
Teacher	Why don't they? Why do men know what to do then?
Johnny	Men just look.
Teacher	How do they know what to do?
Johnny	They just look with a torch.
Teacher	Don't you think they learned how to do it once? Lisa says that ladies can learn how to fix cars.

This kind of discussion, handled carefully, can help young children to share their views and listen to other people's points of view.

Using fairy tales

There is nothing constant about the way fairy tales are passed on through our culture and history. Stories change to meet the needs of each new generation and are still changing now, as storytellers and writers meet the needs of their audiences. Children will almost certainly not know this, and it's worth talking to them about the way tales were written down in the Victorian period so that little girls could identify with good, kind, passive princesses (who were also quite often good at housework too) and boys could see themselves in the guise of heroic, all-rescuing princes. Classroom activities can help children to look at these traditional character roles in order to explore their own personal needs. They can also usefully compare traditional tales with modern retellings and brand-new fairy stories written for children today.

You might begin by reading a well-known version of 'The Sleeping Beauty' and then dividing the children into groups to discuss the characters of the prince and princess. You could follow this up by reading a different version of the story, for example, 'The Sleeping Prince',[29] an old Spanish folktale:

> A princess sat sewing at her window seat. It was snowing outside and as she pricked her finger the blood fell on the window sill. A bird sang in the garden below and told the princess of a handsome prince who lived far away and who was under a magic spell. He and everyone in his castle lay fast asleep and only woke up once a year. If he should see a maiden when he woke up, then the spell would be broken.
>
> The princess resolved to find him and set out through the forest. She wandered for many days and finally the North Wind told her that the prince she was seeking was asleep in a castle nearby, but she must take care since it was guarded by two fierce lions; but if she threw two white roses in front of them they would not harm her.
>
> The princess plucked two white roses and bravely walked towards the castle. As she reached the gates the lions got ready to pounce on her, but she threw the roses at them and they lay down and let her pass.
>
> She found everyone asleep in the castle and when she reached the royal bedroom she saw the handsome prince asleep on his bed. She tried to wake him but could not. For many days and nights she sat by his bed.
>
> Suddenly, one night, on the stroke of midnight, he awoke. He was overjoyed to see a maiden, since the spell was now broken. The prince and princess fell in love and were married. They lived happily for the rest of their lives.

You could then ask the children:

- to compare the roles of the prince and princess in both accounts
- to decide which of the versions they liked the best and why.

Other suggestions for classroom activities include asking the children:

- to read a modern fairy story ('Petronella',[30] for example) and then discuss in groups why they think the author has written the story in this way, with an intelligent, good-humoured and infinitely sensible princess, and a slightly less-than-capable prince;

- to read a modern picture-story book of a fairy tale (for example, *The Paper Bag Princess*[31] or *Prince Cinders*[32]) and then write their own version of a picture-story book for younger children in which the main female and male characters do not act in the conventional roles found in traditional fairy tales;

- to learn to *tell* their favourite fairy tale. After practising with a friend, they could tell their story to younger children in the school or to a nursery class.

Jill and the Beanstalk

In groups, act out the story with all the roles reversed. Jack becomes Jill, his widowed mother becomes Jill's father, the giant would be female and the giant's wife would then become the husband of the giant!

Afterwards discuss in groups what difference this made to the story and the way you had to make the characters behave and speak.

Here are more stories for you to dramatise, with the sexes reversed:

- Teeny Tiny and the Witch Man
- The Three Bears (where mother bear is biggest and strongest and Goldilocks is a boy)
- Little Red Riding Hood (who is a boy; the wolf is female)
- The Three Little Pigs (all female – and a female wolf too)
- The Sleeping Beauty (where she wakes him up).

Can you think of any others?

Tasks for children: *using fairy tales*

Programmes of Study for the National Curriculum

Programmes of Study that are covered by these activities to do with children and their reading:

Speaking and listening

Key Stage 1   The range of activities should include:

- listening and responding to stories – familiar and unfamiliar.

Key Stage 2   Pupils should be given the opportunity to learn how to:

- discuss increasingly complex issues.
- present factual information in a clear and logically structured manner.
- work with or devise an increasing range of drama scripts, taking a variety of dramatic roles.

Reading

Key Stage 1 Activities should ensure that pupils:

● ask and answer questions about what has been heard or read – how characters feel, their motives, the endings of stories.

Key Stage 2 Pupils should:

● be encouraged to respond to the plot, character or ideas in stories, and to refer to relevant passages or episodes to support their opinions.

Writing

Key Stage 1

● Pupils should be asked to write in response to a range of well-chosen stories.

Key Stage 2 Pupils should:

● be helped to understand that non-chronological types of writing can be organised in a variety of ways and so, generally, require careful planning; this might include the presentation of information.
● be helped to increase their control of story form, through their experience of the stories they have read and heard
● discuss the history of writing and consider some of the ways in which writing contributes to the organisation of society, the transmission of knowledge, the sharing of experiences and the capturing of imagination.

▬ *Learning about the media* ▬

The media is highly attractive and influential: television, radio, books, newspapers, magazines, advertising – all exert a powerful force over our lifestyles. Media education in primary schools over the last few years has sought to demystify the media industry by helping children to understand how media choices are made.

The world of comics

Comics are very clearly targeted at boys or girls, and reflect the gender roles that young children take on for themselves. Their use of language, their story lines, their heroes (male and female), and the games and puzzles that form part of the magazines are all part of a gender-package.

I Work in mixed-sex groups and do a survey to find out which comics boys and girls prefer in your school, perhaps by surveying a class each. You could write your findings initially on a tally chart, like this:

Comic	Girls	Boys
Beano	//	++++ ///
My Little Pony	++++ /	/
Teenage Mutant Hero Turtles		++++ //
Superman		++++
Twinkle	///	
Care Bears	////	/
Mask		//

Your chart will tell you which comics are read by boys, and which are read by girls. Report this information back to your class.

Now design a chart to show at a glance which comics are read by girls and boys in the whole school. Report your findings to the school at class assembly time. Try to explain why some comics appeal to boys and some to girls.

2 In groups, look through some popular comics and make a list of the heroes in the stories (male and female). What makes them heroes? Are the male and female heroes alike in any way?

3 Write a comic strip of your own for your class library. It must interest both boys and girls.

Tasks for children: *the world of comics*

Images of women

It is not uncommon for teachers to have to deal with situations in their classes where girls become embarrassed by, and boys giggle at, images of near-naked women in the tabloid newspapers which they have brought from home to use on their painting or glueing tables. There are several ways of handling this situation which can help the children to understand the power of the media and feel more powerful themselves in this situation.

There is no reason why you shouldn't discuss the issue with your class, making sure that everyone's view is represented. Suggest to the children that if they feel strongly they can write and complain. In one such project, a letter of complaint to *The Sun* received the following reply which Zoe and Sharron forwarded to the Press Council in order to pursue their complaint.

Registered Office   **News Group Newspapers Ltd.**   *Registered No. 679215 England*

A Subsidiary of News International Ltd.   Telex: Sunnews 267827

30 Bouverie Street, Fleet Street, London, EC4Y 8DE.   Telephone 01-353 3030

8th October 1980

Dear Zoe

Thank you for your letter.

We can only say to you what we said to another young lady from your school, Sharon Randell. That is, inspite of what you may have been told, there is nothing "rude" about our pictures of unclothed ladies and on occasion men as in the Daily Male feature. The Model girls who pose for the pictures are not being made fun of at all. They are greatly respected for their beauty and every year we get hundreds of letters from girls whose ambition is to have their picture on Page 3 of The Sun.

If we stopped putting these pictures in the paper many of our readers would write and complain - and not all would be from male readers.

Thanks again for your interest in The Sun.

Best wishes

Yours sincerely

Paul Buttle
Picture Editor

Figure 10 *The Sun's* reply to Zoe's letter of complaint

Dear Sir or mrs,

I wrote to the sun and this is a copy of the letter that he sent to me. That's what he thinks.
I think he's rather mean because we get sick of it All the boys pick on the ladies and make fun of them and everyone laughs at them. why would they want to put something like that in?
why don't they put men in?
why do the women let them do it?
I think the women who do it are silly Because they shouldn't show other people what they've got. Could you please tell the. other newspapers to stop putting the pictures in because i get sick of it. Alot of children at our school bring the Sun newspaper in for painting and the boys look at them in stead of using them for painting.
We had a vote on whether more people wanted to stop putting these photographs in the papers or carry on and this was the result.

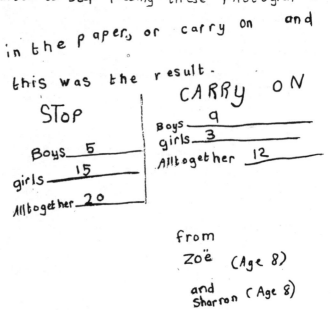

STOP

Boys   5
girls   15
Alltogether 20

CARRY ON

Boys   9
girls   3
Alltogether 12

from
Zoë   (Age 8)
and
Sharron (Age 8)

Figure 11 Zoe and Sharron write to the Press Council

THE PRESS COUNCIL

No. I SALISBURY SQUARE, LONDON EC4Y 8AE

ESTABLISHED 1953
Tel: 01-353 1248

Chairman: F. P. NEILL Q.C.
Director: KENNETH MORGAN O.B.E.

Please quote our reference: R8098

FIRST CLASS
24 Nov 80

Dear Zoe and Sharon,

     Thank you very much for your letter about the pictures in
THE SUN and for sending me a copy of the letter which the picture
editor of THE SUN sent to you.

     I was very interested in your letter and especially that
you and the others in your class went to the trouble of having a
vote about whether you wanted pictures like these to go on being
published in newspapers.

     I think it might be helpful if I told you a bit about the
Press Council. It is a group of about 36 men and women. Half
of them are people who work for newspapers and the other half are
people from all kinds of jobs not connected with newspapers. They
include housewives, teachers, a bishop, an admiral, trade union
members, and people who do different jobs in offices. Together,
under a chairman who is a lawyer, they consider complaints about
what is printed in newspapers. The Press Council will tell the editor
of a newspaper if it thinks something in his newspaper was unfair
or untrue or wrong for some reason.

     It cannot stop an editor from publishing in his newspaper the
things which he thinks should be published and the things he thinks
readers will want to see. It is important that neither the Press
Council nor anyone else should be able to tell an editor what he
must or most not put in his paper, because it is important that
newspapers should be free.

     Most people think that one of the good things about living in
England is that there are lots of different newspapers and most
readers can find one they like.

     Although you and most of the girls in your class may not like the
pictures of women which you see in THE SUN - and other newspapers -
many people do like them because many people buy those newspapers.

Figure 12 The Press Council's response

There are newspapers which do not have pictures of the
kind you object to in them and perhaps when you begin buying
newspapers yourselves you will choose that sort of newspaper.
I think it is a good idea to let people choose for themselves
even if they choose newspapers with things in them that you and
most of the girls and some of the boys do not like.

As long as what appears in a newspaper is not untrue, or
unfair to someone, and does not harm people, it is better that
the newspaper should be free to print it than that anyone
should have the power to stop it doing so.

I am sending you with this letter a leaflet which tells you a
little more about the Press Council.

If I were you I would try to get some plain paper - or
newspapers without many pictures in - for painting lessons!

Yours sincerely,

Kenneth Morgan.

KM/DH   Director

Enc: Leaflet 109.

The power of advertisements

Children are often totally unaware of themselves as a target audience for those who want to exploit their spending power and their enthusiasm for new crazes. One way of introducing the idea of a 'target audience' is to record some advertisements to watch and discuss with your class. Try to choose some that are shown at different times: at half-time in a football match, in the afternoons between TV soaps and at children's TV time. You could then talk with the class about what the advertisement is trying to sell, how it's trying to sell it, and who it's aimed at – men, women, or boys or girls.

I would like to be a barbie doll

Figure 13 The power of advertisements: *when six-year-old Kim grows up she wants to become her own doll*

1 In groups, design your own advert to go on the wall or in the school newsletter for something you want to sell. You will need to decide what the product is, who you want to buy it (man, woman, boy or girl), and how much it will cost.

Now plan the kind of advert for your product that you'd like to see on TV or hear on the radio. Use music or other sound effects. Present it to your class.

2 Look carefully at advertisements for toys. What do they tell you about the people who are trying to sell the toys? Design an advert for a Superman figure that girls would want to buy. Design an advert for a Barbie doll that boys would want to buy.

3 In groups, design and present an advertisement to your class, using sound effects, where the traditional roles of males and females are reversed. Here are some ideas for products:

washing powder
Lego
doll
My Little Pony
lawn mower
Jaguar car
shampoo
washing-up liquid
Michelin car tyre
deodorant
circular saw.

Tasks for children: *the power of advertisements*

Programmes of Study for the National Curriculum

Programmes of study that are covered by these activities on media presentation:

Speaking and listening

Key Stage 1   The range of activities should include:

- securing responses to visual and aural stimuli.

Key Stage 2   Pupils should be given the opportunity to learn how to:

- present factual information in a clear and logically structured manner.

Reading

Key Stage 1   Activities should ensure that pupils:

- make their own books about particular experiences, areas of interest or personal stories.

Key Stage 2 Pupils should:

- be shown how to read different kinds of materials in different ways.

Writing

Key Stage 1 Pupils should:

- undertake a range of chronological writing including . . . letters.

Key Stage 2 Pupils should:

- use writing to learn and to record their experiences in a wide range of classroom activities
- be encouraged to be adventurous with vocabulary choices.

CHAPTER 5

Taking Action in the School

▬ *In the staffroom* ▬

Ideally, teachers in primary schools need to work together to produce a policy document for English that encompasses gender equality and contributes to the school's equal opportunity policy. This is not easy. Policies sometimes take years to formulate – and then have to be constantly updated as ideas are reworked and fresh insights are brought to bear on gender issues.

It is essential for each school to devise an equal opportunities policy that suits its particular needs. There isn't a model policy to adopt and there shouldn't be, because the exciting and sometimes difficult process of change which a school and its community goes through as it formulates its own policy is a crucial part of people's learning and thinking in that area. And of course frequent staff changes mean that there can never be complacency about the nature of the policy and any agreement to it. So-called 'old ground' might be new territory for some. Teachers who have never been involved in professional discussions about gender equality may find the area difficult as, in order to understand what is involved, they will have to examine their own personal and professional behaviour and attitudes. This can be threatening, and some teachers will need a great deal of support over a period of time.

The National Curriculum will not on its own promote equality within schools. Teachers with responsibility for co-ordinating English policy need to work closely with colleagues in planning schemes of work for English which take account of: the activities and experiences to be presented; teaching styles and appropriate groupings of children; the learning needs of girls and boys, including their possible different attitudes to, say, poetry; cross-curricular links; resources and materials (people, space, time, books, films, TV programmes, slides, school visits and so on) and, finally, evaluation and assessment.

With so much to consider it is easy to allow the gender dimension within English to slip away. For this reason it is important to have a strategy which ensures that gender issues are raised at regular intervals; some schools, for example, build a gender component into their termly or half-termly evaluation of a scheme of work, so that it remains a firm part of the agenda. Other schools devise an action plan based on reviewing existing practice, making new policy and developing school-based INSET to support teachers as they implement policy.

One Midlands school first decided to look at the whole area of gender-based equal opportunities about four years ago and, after a series of discussions, the staff were able to agree on a set of general statements about gender issues. This was the first time these statements had been written down. The document was headed: 'Some things we can do in school'. The title itself was tentative and impermanent, as was the document itself, but the process of formulating it was instructive and, once written and agreed, it helped staff to shape practice and develop policy in curricular areas:

Some things we can do in school

1 We should base all our activities on the principle of equality between the sexes and give our boys and girls equal status in school. Our children should be offered the same rights, the same responsibilities and the same expectations in all sections of the curriculum.

2 We should be aware of any school organisation based on gender, e.g. lining up. (When lines are required, children can line up in register order.)

3 We must continue to break down traditional sex-role patterns in school by creating an environment where pupils feel valued, relaxed and able to communicate. We should encourage their involvement in non-competitive, co-operative activities.

4 We should encourage both boys and girls to become autonomous by helping them to show emotions that are positive and constructive in everyday relationships. Boys can be encouraged to show feelings of warmth, sensitivity and generosity; girls can be assertive and positive, firm, decisive and courageous. Above all, we should help children to be aware of the similarities that exist between the sexes.

5 We should be aware of the language of sexism and never use words that denigrate females and emphasise the superiority of males. Beware of using 'he' and 'man' as generics. We must be aware, too, of using language which firmly locates boys and girls in masculine and feminine roles, e.g. boisterous, rough, aggressive, rowdy, fussy, bitchy, giggly, catty, tomboyish.

6 We know that children learn a great deal from the way adults treat each other, as well as from the way they themselves are treated. We must therefore be good role-models for the children – so when, for example, we share tasks in school without regard to hierarchy or sex (e.g. helping to hump the TV up the infant steps!), our supportive attitude to each other is noticed by the children.

7 We must, wherever possible, use non-sexist books and materials. If we do use sexist materials, we should find ways of using them that challenge assumptions and stereotypes.

8 We must focus on the achievements of women in projects and find ways of celebrating successful women, so that our girls have strong role-models put before them.

9 We should find ways of putting girls into responsible roles.

10 We must always be on the lookout for ways of showing males and females in non-stereotyped roles.

11 We should challenge sexist jokes and sexist abuse and take time to discuss with children the negative and damaging effects it has for both males and females.

12 We should appoint a person with responsibility for equal opportunities in the school.

Once the school staff had agreed upon a set of principles there was a feeling that teachers needed time to try to put them into operation. A teacher was appointed to the post of responsibility for equal opportunities but she left the area six months later. When the next post-holder for equal opportunities was appointed she was asked by the headteacher to review existing practice, partly because the head wanted the post-holder to have a clearly defined task, but also because the time was right to move the school forward in its thinking. With the post-holder's help, the staff were able to reflect on their current position. These notes were taken from their meeting:

Reviewing: where have we got to?

Good practice which is already taking place

1 Class registers are alphabetically ordered and are not separated into boys and girls.

2 Class teachers line children up in register order.

3 Children are taught in mixed-sex groups for P.E. and games.

4 Class teachers and educational assistants treat boys and girls alike regarding allocation of time in the home corner.

5 The school management team has both male and female members of staff.

6 There is a male infant teacher. Male Youth Training Scheme workers are placed in the nursery and infant classes.

7 Members of staff have attended equal opportunities courses.

Negative aspects of our school

1 Lunchtime supervisors are all female.

2 There are sexist seating arrangements in the school dining room.

3 A disproportionate amount of teaching time is taken up with the problems that arise from boys' behaviour problems.

4 Girls still do not have an equal amount of computer time.

5 We have not thought out carefully enough the criteria we use for seating and grouping children in the classroom.

6 We still tend to aim our topics/stories at boys to hold their attention.

7 Too many of our books are sexist, either by intent or omission.

The headteacher then asked the post-holders for each major curricular area to devise gender-based policies which responded to both the positive and negative aspects of the statement and which would feed into a whole-school policy. The post-holder for English worked with the equal opportunities post-holder and a working group representing each age phase to produce a set of proposals which would form the basis of a working document. Three main areas were identified: books and resources; media studies and language.

Books and resources

1 We should have a display of anti-sexist books from the National Book League, and remove existing sexist books from libraries.

2 We should invite female authors, illustrators, storytellers and poets into school.

3 We should encourage children to look critically at literature.

4 We should have a 'Horror Box' in the staffroom for collecting sexist literature.

5 We should find better ways of teaching poetry to boys.

Media Studies

6 We should encourage children to look critically at the media (TV, advertising, newspapers, comics, radio, and so on).

Language

7 We should be aware of our use of language (e.g. referring to doctors as 'he'; to humankind as 'mankind', and so on).

8 We must always challenge sexist behaviour and language.

9 We must help children to become aware of themselves as language-users.

10 We need to consider how the 'Knowledge about Language' strand within the National Curriculum can be used to help children learn about language and gender.

These proposals were agreed by the staff and formed the agenda for school-based INSET over one term.

▬ *Reviewing current practice* ▬

Post-holders who are helping staff to review practice might find that colleagues can immediately identify particular areas of the English curriculum that are causing concern. Sharing these concerns will help to focus attention on problems and make it easier to find ways forward. However, teachers who have not been used to reviewing practice could find this area difficult and threatening. Post-holders can help by encouraging staff to concentrate on issues that are to do with children's learning, with the focus at this point on the child rather than on the teacher, such as pupil–pupil talk, or resources. Vague and discursive talk at equal opportunity meetings, for example, can alienate staff who are not committed to formulating and implementing a policy: these people above all need to be included in debate and to see clear progress being made.

If staff are unsure about areas for review, the post-holder might want to suggest areas for reflection, such as:

- whole-class discussion
- organisation of teaching groups
- situations for group learning
- teacher intervention
- teacher response to the use of sexist language
- teacher–pupil talk
- pupil–pupil talk
- books and resources for early reading
- drama
- media studies
- sex-typing in the nursery
- bias in non-fiction books.

Don't try to work on all these fronts at once. If possible, begin with an area that people are specially interested in and identify and promote existing good practice within this area by inviting individual teachers to share their classroom experiences with colleagues. In this way they will know that their skills and knowledge are valued and they will feel more involved in the process of change and growth.

Teachers can collect data on aspects of the area they are reviewing by observing each other's classes with a specific purpose in mind. What they choose to focus on, of course, will depend on their own needs. If school staff have chosen to look at teacher–pupil and pupil–pupil talk in the classroom, for instance, they might decide to collect information about:

- the language behaviour of girls and boys in the home corner
- language used to accompany play with construction toys or dolls
- teacher talk in class discussions
- mixed-sex and same-sex conversations
- single-sex and mixed-sex groups at work on the same task.

It might be possible to raise your own and each others' awareness of the particular area under scrutiny with the help of a checklist or questionnaire for staff to complete. Checklists about language might take this form:

Using non-sexist language

- Does our school have a headmaster, headmistress or headteacher?

- Are there dinner ladies or dining-room supervisors in our school?
- Are there 'Ladies' and 'Gentlemen' signs on our lavatories?
- Do we look for 'strong' boys to move furniture and 'careful' girls to tidy up?
- Do children overhear us talking to other teachers about that 'nice little girl' or that 'difficult boy'?
- Do we praise girls for looking pretty but not for achieving?

Verbal abuse

- Do we have a consistent approach to dealing with verbal abuse throughout the school?
- Do we challenge sexist comments from either sex in the classroom and staffroom?

Dealing with children rather than boys and girls

- Do we arrange registers alphabetically?
- Do the children line up in same-sex lines?
- Do we praise and reprimand boys and girls in different ways?
- Do we spend more time talking to boys and answering their questions and demands?
- Do we expect boys and girls to reach similar standards of presentation of work?

The process of drawing up your own checklist is valuable in itself because it requires a certain intellectual rigour and forces people into explicitness. If you do write your own checklist or questionnaire, decide exactly which areas you want to know more about and don't be tempted to include too much. Share the findings with each other and anyone else you think ought to know: the children themselves, the governing body, parents, and so on.

At this time you could also usefully arrange meetings with other schools to share learning and ideas, and for mutual support. Try to make sure you keep up-to-date with current research in the area you are reviewing. Ask an adviser or consultant to spend time with you and with members of your group who want some theoretical knowledge and need to look at issues in more depth. Read current literature. You could also encourage teachers with a particular interest in gender studies to study the area in greater depth, perhaps by taking a university course.

While this period of review is taking place there are ways of helping staff to see that change is happening by ensuring that short-term goals are met. Organising events which will interest them and the children, such as a visit from a female storyteller or poet, or an exhibition of non-sexist books, will help to keep morale high.

Reviewing resources

Some schools find that taking a close look at their teaching materials, including books, can be a good place to begin the reviewing process. There are clear goals to aim for and the work involved can help to unite staff – a good starting point, then, for groups of teachers who don't know each other well.

The materials used in the classroom to support the English curriculum – books, workcards, illustrations, TV and radio programmes, computer programmes, posters, and so on, should reflect the school's belief in gender equality and the criteria for selection need to be part of the English and equal opportunities policy.

It will be useful for you to draw up a tell-at-a-glance, gender-based checklist to measure resources. Positive and negative statements might be built around this kind of framework, though this of course is a gross over-simplification and detailed checklists should always be consulted.

Negative statements

- Males are shown to be more important than females (stronger, more intelligent, more creative, and so on).
- Males and females are both portrayed in stereotyped and limiting ways.
- The language is sexist.
- The central character is male.
- The heroine, if there is one, is beautiful, passive and dependent. Other women are ugly and scheming.
- The illustrations reflect the same bias.

Positive statements

- The central character is female.
- Males and females are depicted as warm, intelligent and sensitive human beings.
- There is no sexist language. 'He' is never used to refer to 'she'. 'Man' and 'men' never include women.
- The author is female.
- The illustrations reflect a similar openness.

Decisions need to be made about what to do with sexist material. You can throw it out, take it home and keep it for a souvenir of a bygone age, or perhaps hide it at the back of a cupboard and hope that no one will ever find it. More positively, you might decide to use some parts of the material creatively with a group of children to help them look at books and other materials in a new way. This can be particularly valuable if the material or book was written at a time when attitudes were different; older children especially can learn a great deal about the way values are transmitted through language.

But there can be no simple formula for using non-sexist materials in the classroom; children will not automatically learn to confront their own sexism simply because they are taught with materials considered to be non-sexist. How they are used is crucial, and teachers will need to try out and share ideas with colleagues.

Planning school-based INSET

When a school has completed its review of current practice it will need to define its own pathway towards the formation, implementation and evaluation of its equal opportunities policy, taking into account its own needs and the timetable and priorities it has set out for itself in its school development plan.

A written policy statement has symbolic importance as a public statement of intent. It can also be used as a measure of how well a school is doing in implementing equal opportunities. But real policy, whether agreed or not, is what happens in practice everyday in each classroom in the school. For this reason it is vital for teachers to share ideas and practice on a regular basis in INSET sessions so that good practice can be disseminated and ideas celebrated and evaluated. In this way policy can stay constantly under review.

Many of the ideas in the previous section, 'Reviewing current practice', can be used in school-based INSET, but now the focus will be different: instead of looking at problems, teachers will be seeking to bring about change through their practice. They should be able to see a clear distinction between these two objectives, and for this reason they need to be kept closely in touch with development plans.

It is important for staff to know when equal opportunities INSET will take place through the year, so that they can think and plan ahead. INSET might take the form of:

- a series of after-school meetings (if so, how many will there be?)
- a Teachers' Day
- a residential weekend.

Curriculum post-holders need to consult with the equal opportunities post-holder and the senior management·team to decide on the form and content of each meeting, based on their knowledge of the school's needs. At a time of colossal change, and with so many pressing needs on each school, it is vital that this planning should be carried out methodically, so that the equal opportunities dimension of each curricular area can be considered and developed. If the planning is not well thought-out then this won't happen. Haphazard and unplanned INSET, however well-intentioned and inspirational, is an annoyance to hard-pressed teachers and, in such a context, good ideas can be doomed to failure.

Involving parents

Schools who have invited parents to take part in discussions about aspects of equal opportunities have found that many have shown a keen interest in this area. Different opportunities will arise, of course, as schools discuss their own needs; one school which had discipline problems over the lunch-time period invited parents to oversee children's games – more adults meant that a greater variety of games and play space could be offered to children, and a small sum of money was guaranteed for payment by the local Community Education Project; other schools have invited parents and parent-governors to training days and workshop sessions.

Another inner-city primary school decided to review its criteria for selecting books as part of its English and language policy; a working party of teachers was set up, and parents were invited to join the group. The teachers designed a poster and each child took a copy home (Figure 14). A small group of parents arrived for the first meeting, and it soon became obvious that each person had their own area of concern about bias in books: the presentation of black people, images of girls, the prevalence of sexist language. Interesting questions were raised by parents at this initial meeting too: what right have teachers to tell children what books to read and not to read? Isn't it better for children to make their own choices? Should He-Man annuals be allowed at home and at school? Have we any right to tamper with nursery rhymes and fairy tales – after all, they are part of our cultural inheritance, so isn't it right that children should continue to know and love them? Important questions like these were raised and discussed at length in a supportive atmosphere where parents and teachers felt comfortable enough to express their opinions.

Figure 14

The working party met six times over one term. After the first meeting each parent chose a book to take home to examine for possible bias. They returned the following week with comments and suggestions. One thing that soon became clear was that it was impossible for the group to find a book that did not offend someone; and what offended one person was not offensive to another. One parent gallantly offered to write a book that was completely without bias but found she couldn't do it. Nothing daunted, parents and teachers sorted and re-classified some books, and discarded others. By the end of term they felt they had learnt a great deal about bias and were ready to share their learning with others. The success of this group's experience shows what can be achieved by involving parents from the outset in an important area of equal opportunities policy in a school.

Schools who have not had this kind of contact with parents might feel justifiably nervous about such a level of parental involvement, where parents are not only given a voice in curricular matters but are taken on as partners in learning. Post-holders who are interested in working with parents in this way could raise the issue with colleagues and form a small group of committed people to do a specific task within the equal opportunities brief. If the task is one which is seen to help the school, then staff who are less confident of working in partnership with parents, might be helped towards a different understanding of teacher–parent relations.

Post-holders who are still relatively inexperienced themselves, but who feel they want to work with parents, could again find an area that isn't threatening and invite parents into school. The task might at first be one of helping – mending books, perhaps, or looking after the library – and then, as the post-holder gets to know the parents better, opportunities might be found for joint parent–teacher activity where everyone can become learners in a joint enterprise.

▬ *The role of the Governing Body* ▬

Some schools have always traditionally involved governors in policy-making decisions; others have been more cautious. However, recent legislation now means that all schools have a responsibility to have policy statements approved by governors, and it is worth remembering that the governing body has a statutory duty under the Sex Discrimination Act of 1975 to ensure that equal opportunities are provided within their school.

The Equal Opportunities Commission recommends that one governor should have a special responsibility for monitoring equal rights for children and teachers; it recommends setting up a working party of governors, teachers, parents and officers of the local education authority to formulate a policy for their school[33]. In some local authorities, schools are now including a section in their school brochure which tells parents how equal opportunities are promoted within the school.

In reality many school governors take the lead from the headteacher and staff. When equal opportunities is considered important by the school, and matters are discussed with governors, then there is much more likelihood of policy and practice receiving their urgent attention. If issues are not raised by the school, then it is likely that governors, being busy people, will not see equal opportunities as a major part of their brief, unless they are asked to deal with a complaint brought by either a parent or teacher.

Governors themselves will need to think their way through to agreeing a policy. Some will already have strong opinions: 'It's important to let boys play in the Wendy House,' says one governor, 'but I know a school where they're not allowed in.' Clearly she has thought through her views and has a strong commitment to equal opportunities. She added,'You'd be surprised at some of the things that are said at our governors' training sessions. Some heads and governors make it quite clear that they don't want men teachers, especially with the little ones.'

One governor was concerned that the annual school play showed girls and boys in stereotyped roles but felt unable to mention this to the headteacher and staff. 'I've got to learn ways of talking to the head about certain things so she knows I'm supportive, so I can talk about things that aren't right', says this governor, thoughtfully.

In my experience governors do not want to pry; they are interested in supporting their school and getting the best for the children. Clearly if they have thought about gender issues they will be uncomfortable when they see practices in school that reinforce sex-typing – children lining up and sitting in single-sex rows; the generic use of 'he' and 'his' on school policy documents; the exclusion of boys from the home corner. It is for the school to take the initiative and invite governors to share in the formulation of policy, so that they can feel fully involved, and support their school if necessary.

Conclusion

Making equal opportunities work for the English curriculum demands time, commitment and energy on the part of all those concerned with identifying and implementing change. An equal opportunities policy for English is not simply a document written and approved by all, though the writing of such a policy document might well be part of long-term planning; the policy is better thought of as a continuing process where stereotypes are challenged and people are confronted with alternatives for living and being in all kinds of imaginative ways. Chapters 3 and 4 have shown that there is plenty of opportunity to do this within the Programmes of Study for English in the National Curriculum.

A gender-based policy for English teaching in the primary school has to translate the wide brief offered in the Programmes of Study into creative classroom practice. The policy has to pay attention to resources and to involve parents and governors at appropriate times. The teachers who work with most success seem to be those who set short-term goals for themselves within the wider framework of their commitment to equal opportunities: they make changes in the home corner; they invite parents to help with book selection; they help their children to think about what media images mean. In other words, after analysing their children's needs, they decide on a focus and a timescale and look for positive results from each venture. Their motivation is high because they see the results of their planning; they learn and share together and involve parents and governors whenever they can.

Outside influences on children are strong and there is clearly no room for complacency in our schools; but neither is there room for pessimism. Schools can and do make a difference to children's lives. Teachers who are working within the framework of the National Curriculum can also be at the forefront of social change. What is needed now is their continued commitment to make this happen in their classrooms.

Notes

1 *A Framework for the Primary Curriculum*, No. 1 (National Curriculum Council, 1989), p. 1

2 *English for ages 5 to 16*, (Department of Education and Science and the Welsh Office, 1989), Section 11.2

3 Jean Jacques Rousseau, *Emile* (1762); trans. Barbara Foxley, (Everyman Library, 1957)

4 Mary Wollstonecraft, *A Vindication of the Rights of Woman* (London, 1792; repr. W. W. Norton & Company, 1967) pp. 42 – 43

5 *ibid*. p. 168

6 W. Thompson, *Appeal of One-Half of the Human Race, Woman, Against the Pretensions of the Other Half, Men, To Retain Them in Political, and Thence In Civil and Domestic Slavery* (Longman, 1825; rpr. Virago, 1987)

7 *The Poems of Coventry Patmore*, F. Page, ed. (Oxford U. P., 1949)

8 A. Lurie, *Clever Gretchen and Other Forgotten Folktales* (Heinemann, 1980), pp. xi, xii

9 S. de Beauvoir, *The Second Sex* (Cape, 1953). Originally published as *Le Deuxième Sexe*, 2 vols, (Librairie Gallimard, 1949)

10 B. Freidan, *The Feminine Mystique* (Penguin, 1965), p. 13

11 E. Fisher, 'Children's Books: The Second Sex, Junior Division' in J. Stacey, S. Bereaud, J. Daniels (eds.), *And Jill Came Tumbling After* (Dell Publishing, 1974)

12 G. Lobban, 'Sexist Bias in Reading Schemes' in M. Hayles (ed.), *The Politics of Literacy* (Writers and Readers Publishing Co-operative, 1977)

13 R. Stones, *'Pour out the cocoa, Janet': sexism in children's books*, Schools Council Programme 3 (Longman, 1983)

14 K. Clarricoates, '"Dinosaurs in the Classroom" – a re-examination of some aspects of the "hidden" curriculum in primary schools' in *Women's Studies Int. Quarterly*, Vol. 1, 1978, pp. 353–364. Repr. in M. Arnot and G. Weiner (eds.), *Gender and the Politics of Schooling* (Hutchinson, 1987)

15 *The School Curriculum* (Department of Education and Science, 1981)

16 V. Walkerdine, 'Sex, power and pedagogy' in *Screen*

Education, 38, 1981, pp. 14–23, Repr. in M. Arnot and
G. Weiner (eds.), *Gender and the Politics of Schooling*
(Hutchinson, 1987)

17 E. B. White, *Charlotte's Web* (Puffin, 1969)

18 H. Minns, 'Girls don't get holes in their clothes: sex-typing in
the primary school' in *Alice in Genderland* (NATE, 1985),
pp. 23–24

19 Julia Hodgeon co-ordinated a project on sex-differentiation
in the early years. It was funded jointly by Cleveland L.E.A.
and the Equal Opportunities Commission. See also her
article 'A Woman's World', in *Alice in Genderland* (NATE,
1985)

20 This rhyme is quoted in E. Grugeon, 'The Singing Game: An
Untapped Competence' in M. Meek and C. Mills (eds.),
Language and Literacy in the Primary School, (The Falmer
Press, 1988). Elizabeth Grugeon's recent important research
into girls' singing games and rhymes adds a new social and
cultural dimension to our understanding of this area. See also
her article: 'Underground Knowledge: what the Opies
missed', in *English in Education*, Vol. 22, No. 2., Summer
1988.
    For collections of singing games and children's rhymes,
see: I. Opie and P. Opie, *The Lore and Language of School
Children* (Oxford U.P., 1959) and *The Singing Game*
(Oxford, U.P., 1985)

21 For discussion on this point see V. Walkerdine, 'Sex, Power
and Pedagogy' in *Screen Education*, 38, 1981, pp. 14–23.

22 This transcript is discussed by H. Minns, in *Read It To Me
Now!* (Virago Education Series, 1990).

23 For discussion on this point see V. Walkerdine, 'Sex, Power
and Pedagogy' in *Screen Education*, 38, 1981, pp. 14–23.

24 Quoted in *Gender Equality: Five Primary Schools'
Experience of Change* (Coventry Education Department,
1990). Booklet available from: Elmbank Teachers' Centre,
Mile Lane, Coventry, CV1 2NN.

25 *Language Performance in Schools* (Survey by Assessment
and Performance Unit, 1984). This is a report on the 1982
Primary Survey from the Language Monitoring Team at the
National Foundation for Educational Research. It includes
figures on the distribution of reading performance of girls and
boys.

26 J. Rose, *The Case of Peter Pan* (Macmillan, 1984). Rose
discusses the important themes in children's fiction in her book.

27 E.B. White, *Charlotte's Web*. For further discussion of this transcript see H. Minns, 'Girls don't get holes in their clothes' in *Alice in Genderland*, (NATE, 1985).
28 A. Browne, *Piggybook* (Julia Macrae, 1986)
29 'The Sleeping Prince' in *Clever Gretchen and Other Forgotten Folktales* retold by Alison Lurie (Heinemann, 1982)
30 'Petronella' in *The Practical Princess and Other Liberating Fairy Tales* by Jay Williams (Hippo Scholastic, 1983)
31 R. N. Munsch, *The Paperbag Princess* (Hippo Scholastic, 1983)
32 B. Cole, *Prince Cinders* (Collins Picture Lions, 1989)
33 Equal Opportunities and the School Governor (E.O.C., 1985)

Resources

Children's books which challenge male stereotypes

Browne, A., *Willie the Wimp* (Julia Macrae, 1984);
   Willie the Champ (Julia Macrae, 1985);
   Piggybook (Julia Macrae, 1986)
Byars, B., *The Midnight Fox* (Puffin, 1976);
   The Eighteenth Emergency (Puffin, 1976)
Cutler, I., *Meal One* (Piccolo, 1976). Mother and son romp and
   play rough together and love each other to bits.
de Paola, Tomi, *Oliver Button is a sissy* (Magnet, 1983). Oliver
   wants to be a dancer – and finally gets his wish.
   The Knight and the Dragon (Magnet, 1983). They decide not
   to fight each other!
Furchgott, T., *Phoebe and the Hot Water Bottles* (Fontana,
   1978). Phoebe's father is a single-parent and cares for her
   lovingly.
Graham, Bob, *Crusher is coming* (Collins, 1987)
Harvey, R., and Hilton, N., *Dirty Dave the Bushranger* (Dent,
   1989)
Hughes, S. *Dogger* (Puffin, 1979). Dave loses his toy dog which
   he loves. His family helps him – and all ends happily.
   Helpers (Puffin, 1978). George helps out – as a child-minder
   for the younger children.
Leaf, M., *The Story of Ferdinand* (Puffin, 1967)
Lloyd, T. and Lloyd, B. A., *When will I be a man?* (Peckham
   Publishing Project, 1986). A story about a small boy who
   investigates his future role with the help of his dad.
Ormerod, J., *Sunshine* (Puffin, 1983)
   Moonlight (Puffin, 1983).
   Two picture-stories of a sharing, caring family.
Schoop, J., *Boys don't knit!* (The Women's Press, 1987)
Wahl, J., *Humphrey's Bear* (Gollancz, 1988)
Zolotow, C., *William's Doll* (New York, Harper and Row;
   1972). William embarrasses his father and the rest of his family
   by wanting a doll. His grandmother gives him one and helps
   his family to understand why it's right he should have one.

Children's books with interesting female main characters

Ahlberg, A., *Mrs Plug the Plumber* (Puffin: Happy Families
   series, 1980)

Blance, E., and Cook, A., *Lady Monster has a plan* (Longman, 1978). One of a popular Monster series.

Boyd, L., *The Not-So-Wicked-Stepmother* (Viking Kestrel, 1987).

Burningham, J., *Come Away from the Water, Shirley* (Cape 1977)
Time to get out of the bath, Shirley (Cape, 1978)

Caines, J., *Just us women* (Harper & Row, 1982)

Cole, B., *The Trouble with Mum* (Fontana Picture Lions, 1983)

Cleary, B., *Ramona the Brave* (Hamish Hamilton, 1975)

Darke, M., *A Question of Courage* (Kestrel, 1975). About a girl called Emily and her involvement with women's suffrage.

Fitzhugh, L., *Harriet the Spy* (Collins, 1974). An enterprising girl who logs her friends' every move.

George, J. Craighead, *Julie of the Wolves* (Puffin, 1988). A short novel about an Eskimo girl lost on the north slopes of Alaska.

Hoffman, M., and Burroughes, J., *My Grandma has Black Hair* (Methuen Children's Books, 1989)

Kemp, G., *The Turbulent Term of Tyke Tyler* (Puffin, 1979) Readers only come to realise at the end of the story that Tyke is a girl: teachers and children can discuss why they assumed throughout that she was a boy.

Lindgren, A., *Pippi Longstocking* (Puffin, 1976)

Lively, P., *Fanny and the Monsters* (Heinemann, 1979)

Mahy, Margaret, *The Man Whose Mother was a Pirate* (Puffin, 1976)

McKee, D., *Snow Woman*, (Andersen Press, 1987)

Nesbitt, J., *The Great Escape of Doreen Potts* (Sheba, 1981). A short illustrated novel about the heroine of a local laundrette and her brave, quick-witted escape from capture.

Pearce, P., *The Road to Sattin Shore* (Puffin, 1983). Kate needs to find out what happened to her missing father.

Perl, L., *That Crazy April* (Lions). The story of Cress Richardson, who learns to succeed with her friends, her family – and herself.

Pfanner, L., *Louise builds a home* (Collins, 1988)

Sowter, M., *Maisie Middleton* (Fontana Picture Lions, 1982)

Storr, C., *Clever Polly and the Stupid Wolf* (Puffin, 1967)
Polly and the Wolf Again (Puffin, 1970)
Tales of Polly and the Hungry Wolf (Puffin, 1982)
Three superb collections of stories about Polly, who outwits the wolf on numerous occasions.
Lucy Runs Away (Fontana Lions, 1974)

Ungerer, Tomi, *The Three Robbers* (Methuen, 1977)

Vita, T., *The Ten Woman Bicycle* (Sheba, 1980). A look at how the bicycle liberated women – and at women's co-operation.

Wells, Rosemary, *Noisy Nora* (Collins, 1973)

White, E. B., *Charlotte's Web* (1969). Our hero is a spider – and what a spider!

Wilder, L. I., *Little House on the Prairie* series (1968)

Yeoman, John, *The Wild Washerwoman* (Puffin, 1982)

Folk-fairy tales (including modern stories)

Aitken, A., *Ruby the Red Knight* (Macmillan, 1984). Our hero daydreams about her role and future success.

Binchy, M. *et al.*, *Rapunzel's Revenge* (Attic Press, 1985). Fairytales for feminists. Several well-known authors re-write well-known fairy tales.

Cole, B., *Princess Smartypants* (Collins Picture Lions, 1986)
Prince Cinders (Collins Picture Lions, 1989)
The Clever Princess (Sheba)

Corbalis, J., *The Wrestling Princess and other Stories* (Andre Deutsch, 1989)

Foreman, M., *All the King's Horses* (Hamish Hamilton, 1976)

Haddon, M., *A Narrow Escape for Princess Sharon* (Hamish Hamilton, 1989)

Honey, E., *Princess Beatrice and the Rotten Robber* (Viking Kestrel, 1988)

Kaye, M. M., *The Ordinary Princess* (Puffin, 1981). A resourceful princess who wants to pass unnoticed among her subjects – will she manage it?

Leeson, R., *Never Kiss Frogs* (Hamish Hamilton, 1988)

Lurie, A., *Clever Gretchen and other Forgotten Folktales* (Heinemann, 1980)

Munsch, R., *The Paper Bag Princess* (Hippo Scholastic, 1983)

Ross, T., *Little Red Riding Hood* (Anderson Press, 1982)

Reesink, M., *The Princess who always ran away* (Oxford U.P., 1980)

Riordan, J., *The Woman in the Moon* (Hutchinson, 1985). A collection of stories from around the world of independent and resolute women.

Waddell, M., *The Tough Princess* (Walker Books, 1989)

Williams, J., *The Practical Princess and other Forgotten Fairy Tales* (Hippo Scholastic, 1983)